HAL LEONARD
BASS METHOD

COMPLETE EDITION

Contains books 1, 2, and 3 bound together in one easy-to-use volume

BY ED FRIEDLAND

Edited by Doug Downing

ISBN 0-7935-6382-8

7777 W. BLUEMOUND RD. P.O. BOX 13819 MILWAUKEE, WI 53213

Visit Hal Leonard Online at
www.halleonard.com

BOOK 1

BOOK 2

BOOK 3

THE ELECTRIC BASS

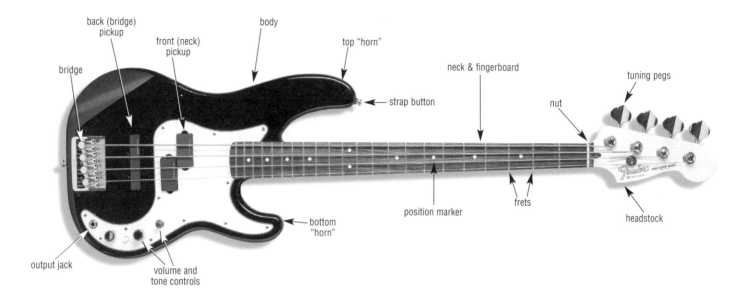

back (bridge) pickup

front (neck) pickup

body

top "horn"

neck & fingerboard

tuning pegs

bridge

strap button

nut

output jack

bottom "horn"

position marker

frets

headstock

volume and tone controls

THE BASS AMP

To hear yourself clearly, it is necessary to play an electric bass through an amplifier. Though there are many different sizes, a simple, self-contained unit ("combo") will work fine. Use a patch cord, or cable, to connect from the output of the bass to the input of the amp. Make sure the amp's volume knob is turned off, or all the way counterclockwise. The tone controls should be set "flat," or at 12 o'clock. Turn on the power, and slowly adjust the volume to an appropriate level. Be careful; too much volume could blow out the speaker!

volume control

tone controls

input jack

power switch

speaker

TUNING

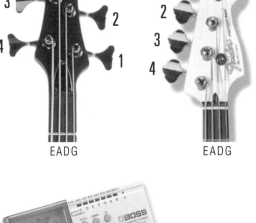

EADG   EADG

To tune your bass, adjust the tuning pegs. Tightening a peg will raise the pitch of a string, loosening a peg will lower it.

The strings are numbered 1 through 4. Follow the instructions below to tune each string in sequence, beginning with the G (1st) string.

USING AN ELECTRONIC TUNER

Electronic tuners have become very affordable, so it's a good idea to have one. There are generally two types available: a "bass" (or "guitar") tuner, which will only read the open strings of your instrument, or a "chromatic" tuner, which will read any pitch. Either will do the job. Plug your bass into the input of the tuner and play your open G string. The tuner will read the pitch and tell you if the string is sharp (too high) or flat (too low). Adjust the tuning peg until the tuner indicates you are in tune. Repeat the process with the D, A, and E strings.

TUNING TO A KEYBOARD

Use the appropriate key on a piano/keyboard to check your open strings.

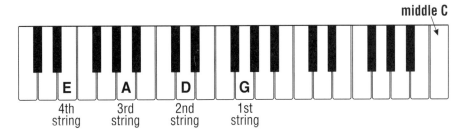

RELATIVE TUNING

Here's another way to tune your bass. It is less accurate, as it assumes that your starting string is in tune—and it is harder for the ear to hear the low pitch of the bass as well as a tuner can—but this method works when there are no other alternatives. It's also a good way to check your tuning.

- Start with your open G string. If there is an accurate G available, use it; otherwise, assume the G string is tuned to the correct pitch.
- Play the D string at the 5th fret, and see if that note matches the open G. Tune the D string up or down until the two notes match.
- Play the A string at the 5th fret; compare it to the open D. Tune the A string up or down until the two notes match.
- Play the E string at the 5th fret; compare it to the open A. Tune the E string up or down until the two notes match.

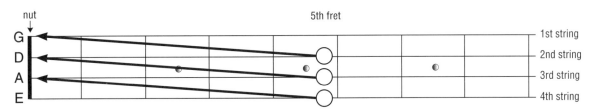

This is called *relative tuning* because the strings are tuned relative to one another.

PLAYING POSITIONS

STANDING

- Buy a comfortable strap between 2½ and 3 inches wide. Leather or woven cotton are good choices. A padded, stretchy neoprene strap will help absorb the weight of the instrument.

- Adjust the strap so that both hands can be comfortable on the bass. With your left arm at your side, bend the elbow, bringing your forearm up. This is your optimal position for the left hand.

- Hold your right arm straight out in front of you at shoulder height, and let the hand hang down naturally. Bend your elbow, and bring your arm in towards your body. That is the optimal position for your right hand.

- Be sure to avoid any extreme bends in either wrist.

TIP: Run the cable under your strap to avoid pulling it out of the jack while standing.

SITTING

- It's best to use a strap while sitting to keep the instrument at the proper height.

- Without a strap, rest the bass on your right leg. It may help to use a small footstool under your right foot.

- Keep your left arm off your leg.

- Angle the neck slightly away from the body.

MUSICAL SYMBOLS

Music consists of two basic elements: **rhythm** and **pitch**. Pitch is notated using a set of lines (and spaces) called a staff. The higher a note appears on a staff, the higher its pitch; the lower a note appears, the lower its pitch. At the beginning of the staff is a clef sign. Bass music is written in the bass clef or "F clef."

STAFF **BASS CLEF**

The two dots in the clef sign surround the line on which the pitch "F" is written; hence the term "F clef."

The musical alphabet uses the letters **A**, **B**, **C**, **D**, **E**, **F**, and **G**. After G, the sequence repeats starting with A. In bass clef, the notes written on the **lines** of the staff are G–B–D–F–A. You can remember this sequence as "Good Boys Do Fine Always." The notes on the **spaces** are A–C–E–G. "All Cows Eat Grass" may help you remember this.

LINES

G   B   D   F   A

SPACES

A   C   E   G

Rhythm, the other basic element of music, is notated using **measures** (also known as "bars"), which contain a set number of beats (the pulse of the music). Each measure is separated from the next by a **bar line**. A double bar line is used to show the end of a section of music. The final bar line is used to show the end of a piece of music.

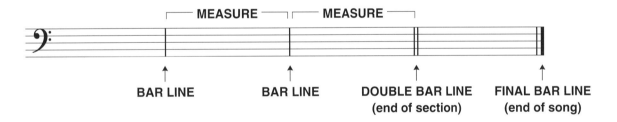

MEASURE   MEASURE

BAR LINE   BAR LINE   DOUBLE BAR LINE
(end of section)

FINAL BAR LINE
(end of song)

The number of beats in each measure is indicated by the **time signature**, which appears at the start of a piece after the clef sign. The time signature looks like a fraction. The top number tells us how many beats there are in a bar, and the bottom number tells us what type of note is to be counted. Most of the examples in this book will be in 4/4 time.

TIME SIGNATURE

→ four beats per measure
→ a quarter note (♩) gets one beat

In the first part of this book, you will see three different kinds of note values. They are:

NOTE VALUES

QUARTER NOTE = 1 beat   HALF NOTE = 2 beats   WHOLE NOTE = 4 beats

RIGHT-HAND TECHNIQUE

FINGERSTYLE

The most common approach for playing electric bass is fingerstyle—i.e., using the index (i) and middle (m) fingers of the right hand to play the strings. The fingers give you a warm, full sound that can be controlled easily by developing touch sensitivity.

- Let your fingers hang comfortably, straight over the strings; don't curl them.
- Start by resting the tip of the thumb gently on the pickup.
- Using the fleshy pad of your finger, place it on top of the string.

E STRING

Gently push down and across the top of the E string, letting your finger come to rest against the pad of the thumb. Alternate strokes between the index and middle fingers. Repeat this until you feel comfortable. Play lightly; too much force will give you a distorted sound.

Fingers: i   m   i   m

right-hand position

A STRING

Move your finger to the A string. Push down and across the string, letting your finger come to rest against the E string at the end of the stroke. Alternate fingers; repeat several times.

Fingers: i   m   i   m

end of fingerstroke

D STRING

Drop your thumb to the E string. Move your finger to the D string, push down and across, letting your finger come to rest against the A string. Alternate fingers and repeat.

Fingers: i   m   i   m

muting the E string

G STRING

Drop your thumb onto the A string, and make it lean against the E string. This mutes both strings to prevent unwanted ringing. Put your finger on the G string. Push down and across the string, letting your finger come to rest against the D string. Alternate fingers and repeat.

Fingers: i   m   i   m

TIP: As you alternate fingers, place each finger down for the next stroke just slightly ahead of time, to mute the previous note. This will give you a more controlled bass sound.

muting the E and A strings

PICK STYLE

Pick style produces a clear, distinct sound, and is a very popular technique for playing rock bass. While most bassists tend to use their fingers, pick style is a good skill to have.

The thickness of the pick will affect the tone: A thin pick may be too floppy to produce a strong tone; a heavy pick may not be flexible enough. See what gauge feels right to you.

- Curl your index finger and place the pick on it, letting just the tip stick out.
- Place your thumb over the top of the pick, holding it securely—but not too tightly.
- Make sure the pick is flat against the string; don't use the edge of the pick.
- Rest your pinky against the face of the bass, or on the lower edge of the pickup.

The pick can be used to play **downstrokes** (⊓) and **upstrokes** (∨). The downstroke has a strong attack and works well for hard rock. Play the previous examples again, this time with a pick, using downstrokes (⊓). Use a light wrist motion with a little bit of forearm movement.

Downstrokes:

TIP: To get a full sound from each string, make sure the pick connects fully; let the pick "travel through" and come to rest against the next string after the stroke. Be careful, however, not to play too hard (especially on strings D and G); overplaying can make the string "flap out," producing a weak tone.

> **NOTE**: While you will eventually develop a preference, it's important to play both fingerstyle and pick style to be a well-rounded bassist. Readers are encouraged to learn fingerstyle first—as it presents many unique challenges to the beginning player—and then, at a later time, to try pick style. Any example can be played either fingerstyle or with a pick.

LEFT-HAND TECHNIQUE

Now it's time to start using the left hand. The fingers are numbered 1 through 4 as shown.

1-2-4 FINGERING SYSTEM

The 1-2-4 fingering system allows us to keep the hand relaxed and comfortable, particularly when playing in the lower regions of the bass where the frets are farther apart. Start with the pad of your thumb in the middle of the neck; make sure it doesn't stick up over the top. The thumb is positioned between the first and second fingers.

- Place your first finger directly behind the 1st fret of the E string, pressing down lightly.
- Place your second finger on the 2nd fret.
- Place your fourth finger on the 3rd fret.

1st position

Notice that we have access to three frets—this is called a **position**. We'll study three playing positions in this book: 1st position (with the index finger at the 1st fret), 2nd position (with the index at the 2nd fret), and 3rd position (index at the 3rd fret).

TIP: Keep your left hand relaxed when you play. Never forcibly stretch your hand or hold a position that feels strained.

2nd position

3rd position

OPEN-STRING EXERCISES

The following exercises are played on the open strings and will help you with basic rhythms, fingerstyle technique, and crossing the strings. Here are the notes for the open strings as written on the staff.

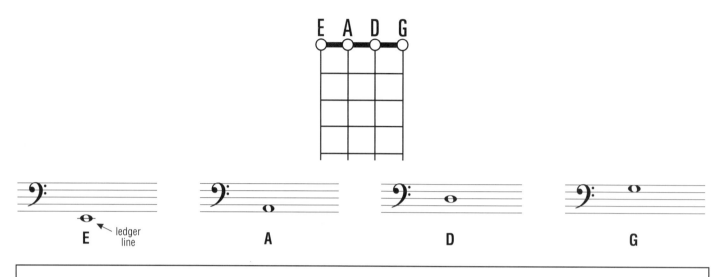

The open E string is written on an added line below the staff, called a **ledger line**.

Each exercise below is played on a single string. Count the rhythms out loud at first, and then play them. As you play, concentrate on alternating between index (i) and middle (m) fingers, as shown.

When playing fingerstyle, the most important thing to remember is to alternate fingers. Once you get used to it, this technique allows you to play notes quickly and easily. You may begin your alteration with either finger—index or middle. Try playing the above exercises again, beginning with "m" instead of "i."

Now let's try playing on more than one string. These exercises move *up* the open strings. Continue to alternate fingers as you move up from one string to the next. Remember to let your fingers "travel through" on each stroke.

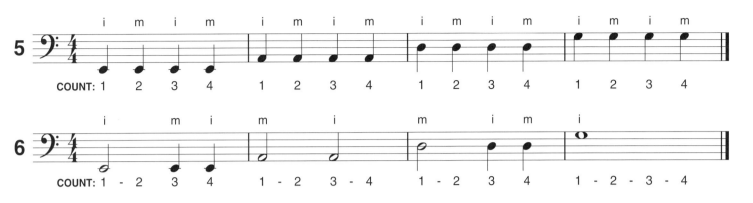

THE RAKE

When moving *down* a string, use the same finger to play both strings—this is called the **rake technique**.

The idea is to use as little effort as possible to get from one string to the next. The rake actually helps keep your right hand relaxed as you move down to the lower string.

Try these exercises moving down the open strings. (Use your left hand to mute the higher open strings.)

This example mixes ascending and descending motion through the strings. It starts on "m," but you could also switch and begin with "i." Remember: When crossing to a higher string, alternate fingers; when crossing to a lower string, use the same finger (the "rake technique") on both strings.

NOTES ON THE E STRING

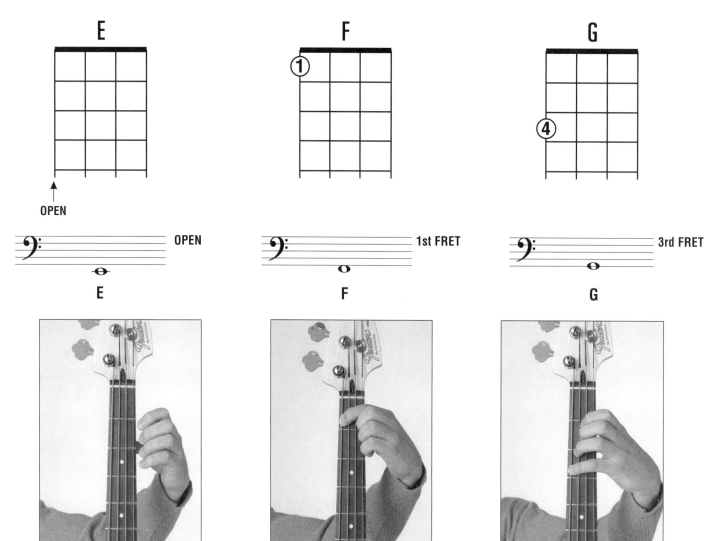

These notes are in **1st position**, with the first finger of the left hand on the 1st fret. Here are a few tips:

- Place your finger directly behind (not on top of) the fret.
- Experiment with different amounts of pressure; it takes less than you think.
- Keep each note ringing until you're ready to play your next note.

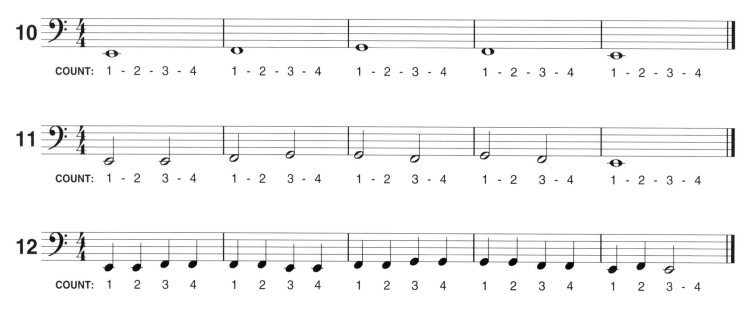

Say the names of the notes out loud while you play, like "E... F... G... F... (etc.)". Remember to alternate i and m fingers in the right hand as you play.

This example skips a space when going from E to G.

Practice keeping the count going on your own.

This next example is 8 measures long. When you reach the end of the first line, continue on to the second line without a pause.

LITTLE ROCK

KINDA FOLKY

MORE NOTES ON THE E STRING

These notes are shown in **2nd position**, with the first finger of the left hand on the 2nd fret.

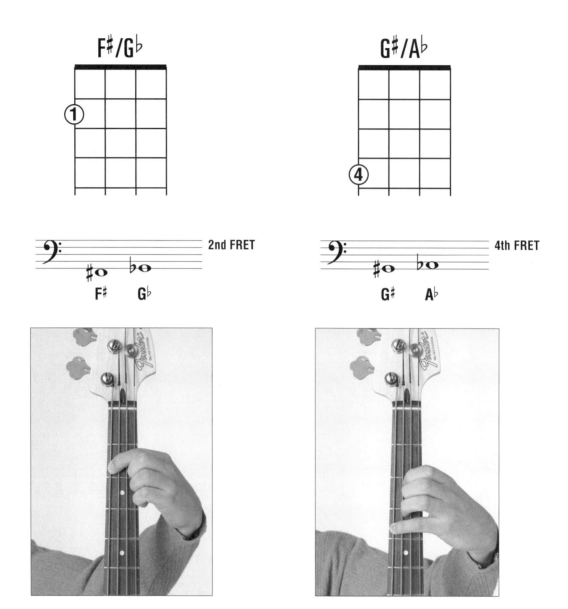

Why does each note above have two different names? Read on...

So far, the notes you have learned have all been **natural notes**—they have a letter name, and that's all. Notes that occur in between natural notes have names with sharps (♯) or flats (♭) next to them.

- When you go up one fret from a natural note, its name becomes **sharp** (♯). For example: Play 1st fret F, then move up to the 2nd fret. That note is called F-sharp (F♯).

- When you move down one fret from a natural note, the name becomes **flat** (♭). For example: Play 3rd fret G, then slide down to the 2nd fret. That note is now called G-flat (G♭).

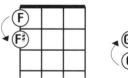

You just noticed that the 2nd fret on the E string has two different names: When you move up from F, we call it F♯; when you move down from G, we call it G♭. That is called an **enharmonic equivalent**.

In written music, a sharp (♯) or flat (♭) placed in front of a note affects every note on the same line or space in that measure. It is automatically cancelled out in the next measure.

LOOKIN' SHARP

A **natural sign** (♮) cancels a previous sharp or flat. In this example, the G natural is played with the second finger.

In the above example, the natural sign "cancels" a sharp from the previous measure. Though not strictly necessary, this helps to avoid any confusion over the intended pitch. This is known as a **courtesy accidental.**

THE SHIFT

In order to play *all* the notes on the E string comfortably, you need to learn how to shift from 1st position to 2nd position. You can shift on any finger: Play the first note, then lighten up on the pressure and slide your hand up or down one fret. Try the following examples, each of which shifts using a different finger.

NOTES ON THE A STRING

A
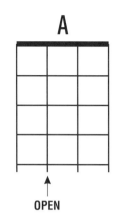

B
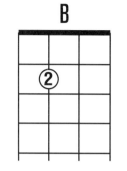

C
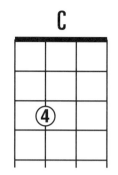

OPEN

 OPEN

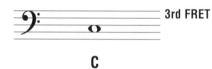 2nd FRET

3rd FRET

A

B

C

These notes are in 1st postion. Remember to say the note names out loud as you play.

Practice slowly, to get the notes securely under your fingers. When you feel comfortable with an example, gradually increase the speed.

YOU GO, SLAV

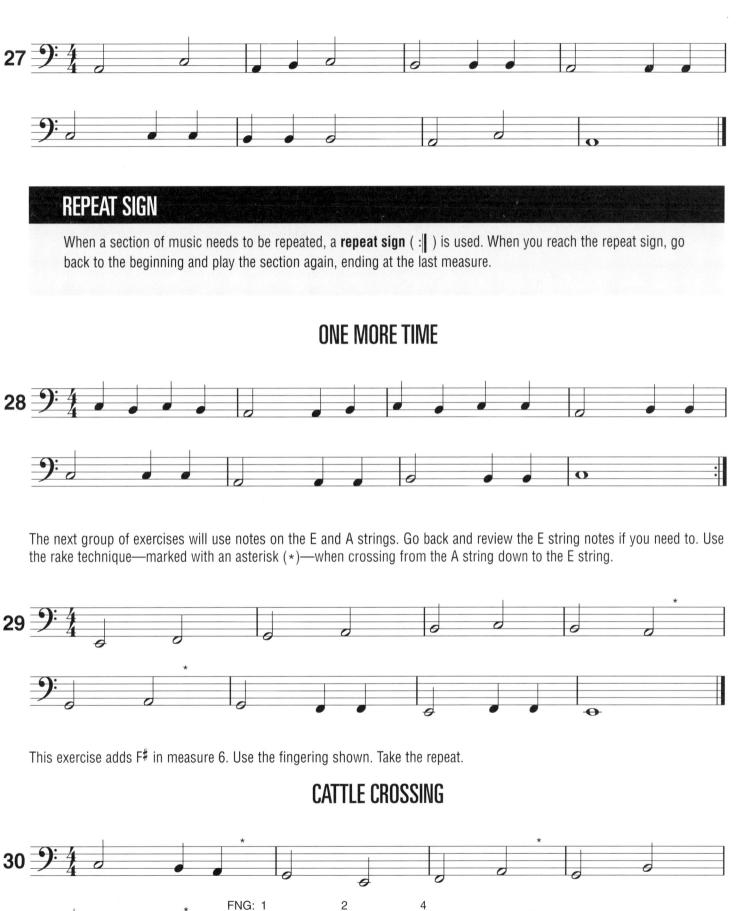

REPEAT SIGN

When a section of music needs to be repeated, a **repeat sign** (:||) is used. When you reach the repeat sign, go back to the beginning and play the section again, ending at the last measure.

ONE MORE TIME

The next group of exercises will use notes on the E and A strings. Go back and review the E string notes if you need to. Use the rake technique—marked with an asterisk (∗)—when crossing from the A string down to the E string.

This exercise adds F♯ in measure 6. Use the fingering shown. Take the repeat.

CATTLE CROSSING

MORE NOTES ON THE A STRING

Just like the E string, the A string has notes that occur in between the natural notes.

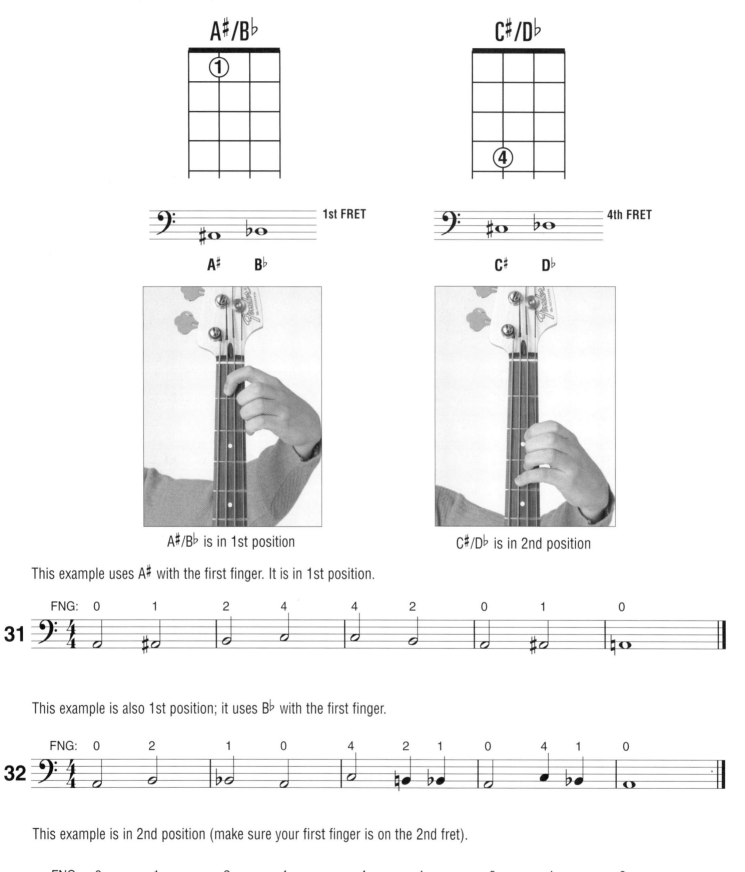

A#/B♭ is in 1st position

C#/D♭ is in 2nd position

This example uses A# with the first finger. It is in 1st position.

This example is also 1st position; it uses B♭ with the first finger.

This example is in 2nd position (make sure your first finger is on the 2nd fret).

THE FINGER ROLL

A special technique for the left hand is the **finger roll.** This helps you when playing notes on adjacent strings located at the same fret. The goal is to cross smoothly from one string to the next. To do this when moving from a lower to a higher string, play the note on the lower string using the tip of the finger (with the small knuckle slightly bent); then, flatten the knuckle and roll your finger across, playing the note on the higher string with the pad of the finger.

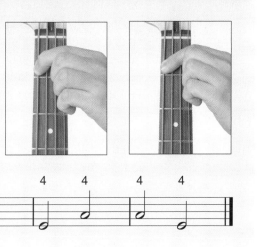

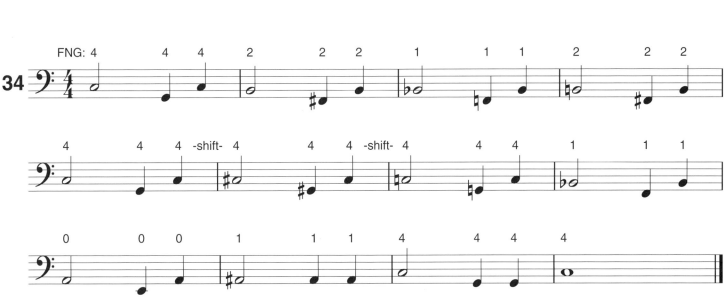

This example thoroughly works the finger roll on all fingers. Observe the position shifts indicated.

ROLL IT

This 2nd position exercise has several string crossings (and uses A♭ on the way down from open A). In measures 3 and 4, there are finger rolls between G and C.

ROLLY

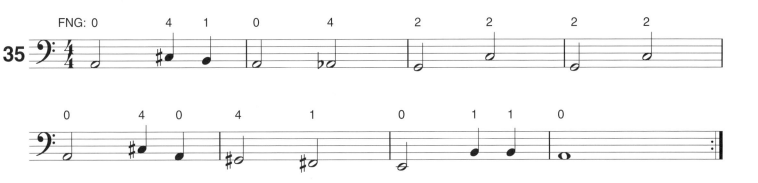

Let's play a longer song form, a **12-bar blues**. This is a common progression in rock, jazz, blues, and many other styles of music. The bass line corresponds directly to **chords** that a guitarist or pianist plays. They will be written above each measure so that your teacher or a friend can play along with you. If you examine the bass line, you will see that when the chord symbol says E7, the bass starts the measure with an E; when the chord changes to A7, the bass plays A; etc. You are playing the *root* of the chord, a very important aspect of functional bass playing.

This line is mostly in 2nd position, with an occasional shift down to 1st position. There are only a few fingerings and shift indications written in to help you. Measure 4 has a pattern called a **triad**—three notes that "spell out" the contents of a chord.

12-BAR BLUES

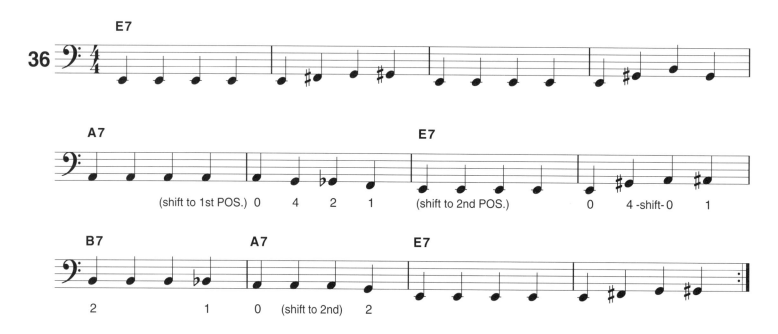

Here is another 12-bar blues. This one changes chords in the 2nd and the 12th measures, a common variation in blues form.

A LITTLE HEAVY

NOTES ON THE D STRING

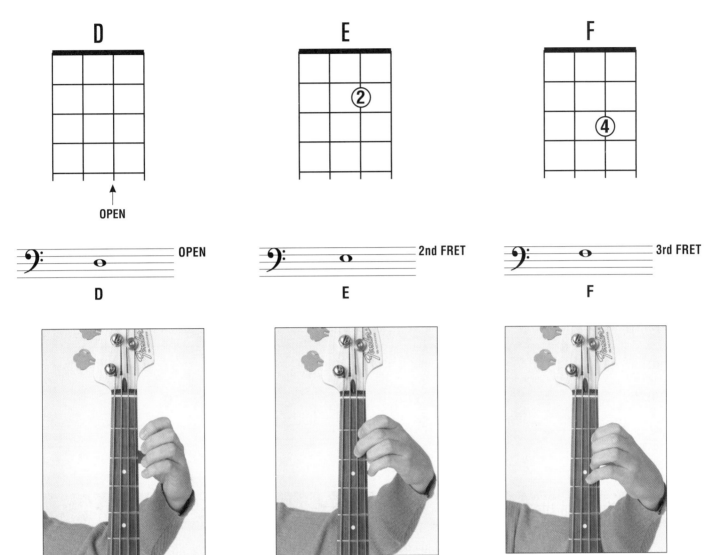

When playing on the D string, remember to drop your right-hand thumb to the E string to keep it muted. Pull straight across with the finger and into the A string. Pick style players: concentrate on your pick accuracy and touch. Don't play the D string too hard.

PRIVATE EYE

This 1st position example crosses the A and D strings. The chord names are included so others can play along. You are playing the root when each chord changes. The symbol "Dm" is for a D minor chord. **Minor chords** sound dark while **major chords** (without the "m") sound happy and bright. Listen for the difference. Watch out for the finger roll in the last measure.

MINOR LEAGUE

1ST and 2ND ENDINGS

The next song has a **1st** and **2nd ending** (indicated with brackets and the numbers "1" and "2"). Play through the 1st ending like a standard repeat sign, and go back to the beginning. The second time through, skip the entire 1st ending and go directly to the 2nd ending section.

This example starts and ends on D; it outlines the sound of the **key** of D. D is the **tonic** or "home base" of the piece. Notice how the bass is not always playing the root when the chords change. You can play other notes that belong to the chord. (This will be explained in depth in Book 2.)

D-LITE

MORE NOTES ON THE D STRING

D#/E♭

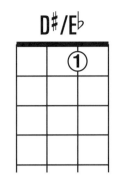

F#/G♭

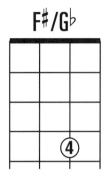

1st FRET

4th FRET

D#   E♭

F#   G♭

D#/E♭ is in 1st position

F#/G♭ is in 2nd position

43

Remember to start in 2nd position.

44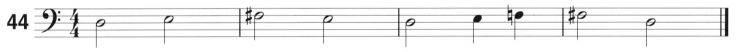

This example shifts between 1st and 2nd position.

45

FNG: 0   1 - shift - 1   4   1   - shift - 1   0   4   2

0 - shift -1   2   4   1   4   0   - shift - 2   1   0

Here are all the notes you have learned so far. Review each note and solidify your understanding of where it is played on the fingerboard and how it is written on the staff.

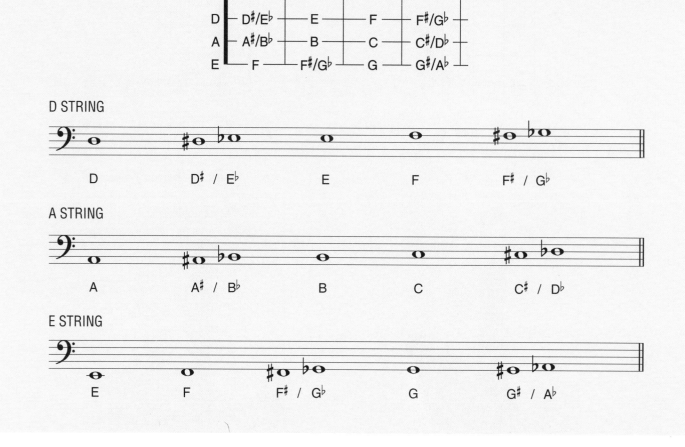

This 2nd position example crosses the three strings you've learned so far. Make sure to follow the 1st and 2nd endings.

CROSSIN' THREE

THE OCTAVE

It's time to look at a musical pattern that is very common in bass playing, the "octave." An **octave** is the same note up or down eight letters in the musical alphabet. For instance, the last two notes in the previous example were both E, but one was high, and one was low—that is an octave.

The octave follows a physical pattern on the fingerboard. From any note on the E (or A) string, move up 2 frets, and across 2 strings. This pattern is consistent throughout the fingerboard.

Fingering an octave (without an open string) requires you to play the low note with the first finger, and the high note with the fourth finger.

For fingerstyle, use your index finger (i) for the low note of an octave and your middle finger (m) for the higher note.

This example uses the octave shape. For fingerstyle, make sure to drop the right thumb onto the E string when making the jump across to play the D string. This example also shifts up with the first finger to 2nd position. Shifting around the octave shape is a very common practice in bass playing.

OCTA GONE

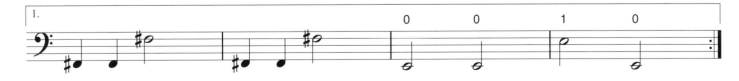

NOTES ON THE G STRING

G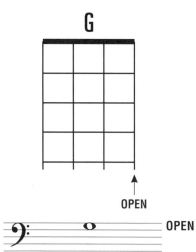

A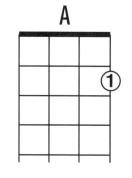

B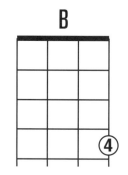

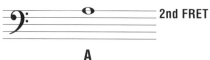
OPEN
G

2nd FRET
A

4th FRET
B

These notes are in 2nd position.

When playing on the G string, make sure your right thumb drops to the A string (muting the bottom two open strings).

This example is in 2nd position and crosses over to the D string. Fingerings are written where necessary.

GEE WHIZ

Now we cross over to the A string. There is a small shift with the 1st finger (indicated simply with "-") from E to E♭ and back.

ALL RIGHT

Now you'll play across all four strings using only the natural notes. Start in 2nd position, and watch for the shifts.

MORE NOTES ON THE G STRING

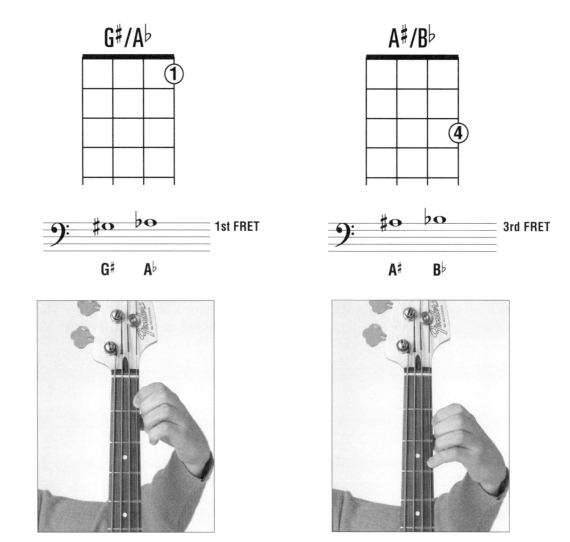

G#/A♭ and A#/B♭ are in 1st position.

This one begins in 2nd position, and then shifts between 1st and 2nd (shifts are indicated with a dash "-").

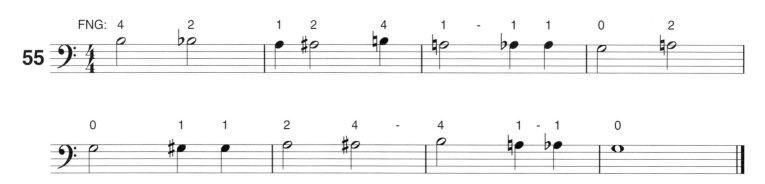

Time for more practice playing across all four strings. This is mostly 2nd position, with one note in 1st position.

ALL FOUR ONE

This one is in 1st position, and uses F as the tonic. There is one shift to 2nd position; fingerings are indicated.

F/X

G major is the tonic. Start in 1st position, but shift in the 6th measure. Use the open D string to move to 2nd position.

MORE OCTAVES

Playing across all four strings, there are more octave shapes available. Here are the new octaves you can play between the A and G strings. Remember that A♯ and B♭ are enharmonic equivalents.

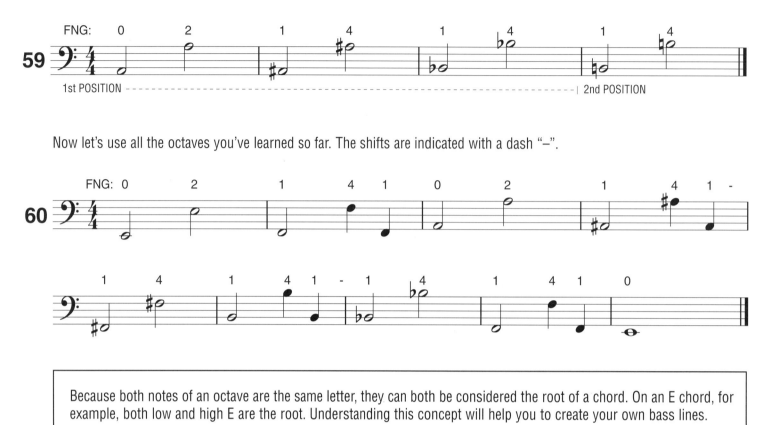

Now let's use all the octaves you've learned so far. The shifts are indicated with a dash "–".

> Because both notes of an octave are the same letter, they can both be considered the root of a chord. On an E chord, for example, both low and high E are the root. Understanding this concept will help you to create your own bass lines.

This 12-bar blues uses the octave on each chord for the bass line. The chords are "seventh chords" (E7, A7, and B7). They are a different type of chord than you've seen, but for now the important thing is to play the root (E, A, and B).

Begin in 1st position; for the B7 chord, shift up to 2nd position. Remember, when playing octaves fingerstyle, the lower note of the octave can be muted with the thumb as you move up to play the higher note on the A or D string. As a general rule, use your middle finger (m) when jumping to the higher note, and your index finger (i) when jumping back down to the low octave.

OCTAVE BLUES

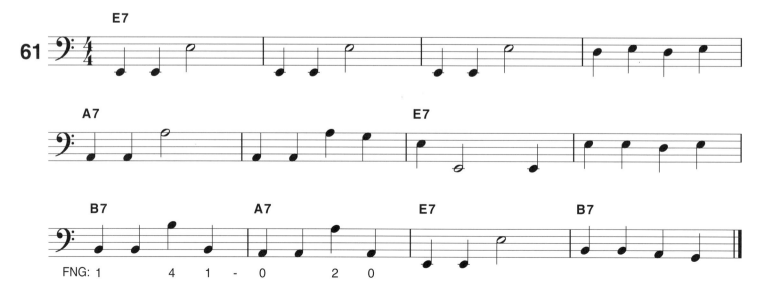

TIES

A **tie** connects two notes of the same pitch. It is used to extend the note value across a bar line, or sometimes within a measure. Play the first note, and hold it for the combined value of both notes.

In this example, some of the chords change on the first beat of a tie. The key is B minor; notice the darker quality of the song.

TAIWAN ON

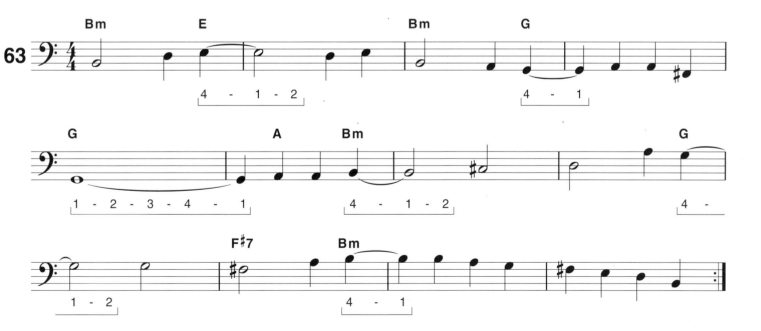

3/4 time has three beats per measure, and the quarter note receives one count.

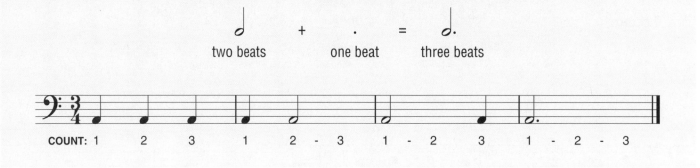

$\dfrac{3}{4}$ → three beats per measure
→ a quarter note (♩) gets one beat

A **dot** after a note extends the note's duration by one-half. A **dotted half note** equals 3 beats.

♩ + . = ♩.
two beats   one beat   three beats

64

This has a country waltz feel, and the tonic is C.

THREE'S A CROWD

65

This example is a gospel-flavored tune. The tonic is F.

TELL IT

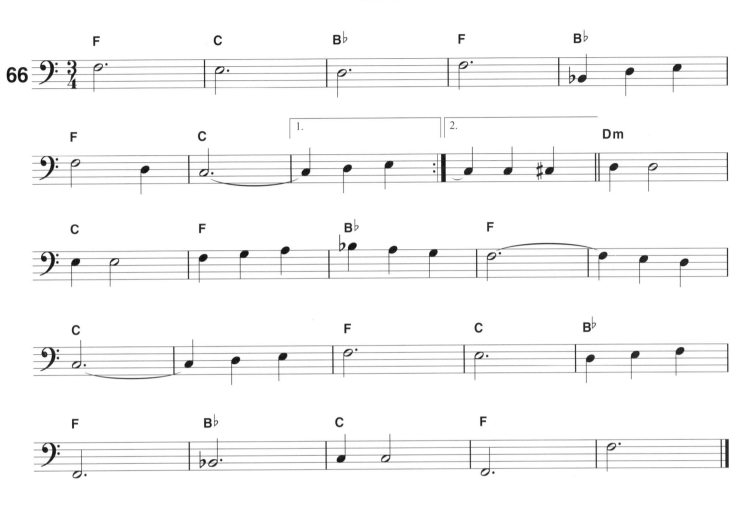

This piece changes time signatures from 3/4 to 4/4. Count your way through—it's easier than it looks, and it's fun. (Hint: Keep your foot tapping on every quarter note!)

CHANGIN' TIMES

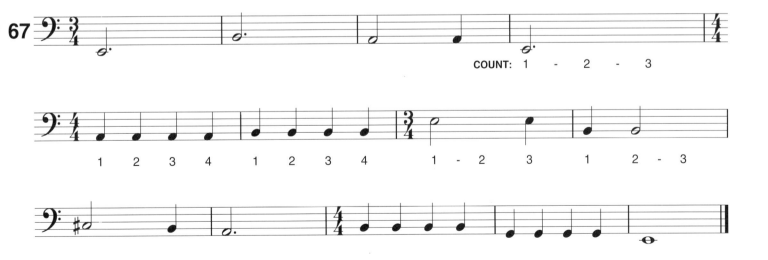

RESTS

Rests are spaces, or silences, in the music, and have specific durations just like notes. In fact, for every note value, there is a corresponding rest of equal value.

It's important to make sure your notes are not still ringing during a rest. Mute the string with your right or left hand, whichever is most convenient.

Although the count is written out only for the first line, keep counting on your own for lines 2–4. Make sure to hold the quarter notes for their full note value.

ROCK 'N' REST

*N.C. = No chord

D.C. al FINE

The marking **D.C. al Fine** is short for "Da Capo al Fine," an Italian phrase meaning, "From the beginning until the end." When you see this marking in a piece of music, go back to the beginning (or "head") of the piece and resume playing until you reach the Fine marking (the "end"), and then stop.

This piece has a jazz-waltz feel. Count through the rests and ties. Note that the root is not always played on each chord.

THREE PLAY

This time, take the D.C. and play the 1st ending back to the beginning; the Fine is the 2nd ending.

EIGHTH NOTES

When you divide a quarter note in half, you get two **eighth notes**. Eighth notes are written separately with flags, or in groups of two or more with beams.

EIGHTH NOTES

In 4/4 and 3/4 time, there are two eighth notes per beat. To count eighth notes, we use the word "and," like this: "1 & 2 & 3 & 4 &." The numbers are called **downbeats**, and the "ands" are called **upbeats**.

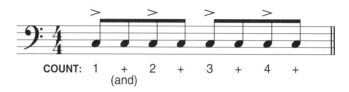

For fingerstyle playing, continue alternating index and middle fingers when playing eighth notes. For pick style playing, alternate downstrokes with upstrokes. Use downstrokes (⊓) on the downbeats and upstrokes (∨) on the upbeats.

Play the following exercise slowly at first. Count aloud, tapping your foot on the downbeats. Keep the count going for yourself on the 2nd and 3rd lines. Then try it again, reversing the fingerings (start with "m").

Here's the same exercise played pick style.

For additional practice, try playing each measure individually in a repetitive loop (you'll need to adjust the right-hand fingerings if playing fingerstyle). Add one measure at a time, and eventually play through the entire exercise.

This tune combines eighth notes with moving lines. Practice keeping the eye moving ahead fast enough to follow the notes. Make sure to count through the rests.

MOVIN' 8'S

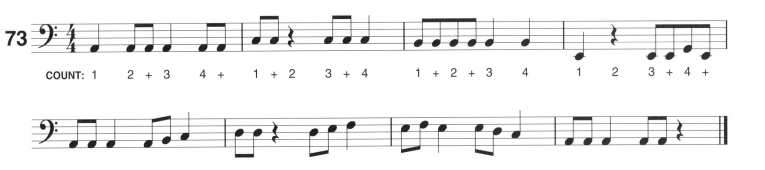

This is in 1st position. F is the tonic or key. Watch for the finger roll with the fourth finger in the last measure.

Notice the use of a consistent idea here; it contributes to a solid bass line. Repetition in the bass part gives a song a feeling of stability and a sense of character.

EIGHT BALL

An **eighth rest** takes up the same amount of space as an eighth note. Eighth rests can occur on a downbeat or an upbeat.

Play this example slowly. Tap your foot on the downbeats, and keep counting out loud through the second line. Practice each measure of this exercise separately until you get comfortable with the feel of it, then string them all together. Fingerstyle, continue to alternate index and middle fingers. Pickstyle, keep downstrokes on downbeats and upstrokes on upbeats.

This example uses a two-measure rhythmic pattern to create a consistent feel. There is a slight variation in measure 7.

ROK GRUV

Here is a cool feel. The "and" of beat 2 gets emphasized.

BOP BOP

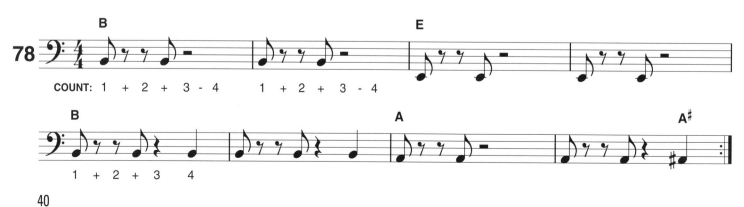

D.C. al CODA

Like "D.C. al Fine," this marking tells you to return to the beginning of the piece. But "al Coda" indicates that you jump to the coda or "tail" section when you reach the appropriate marking. Here is an example with numbered instructions.

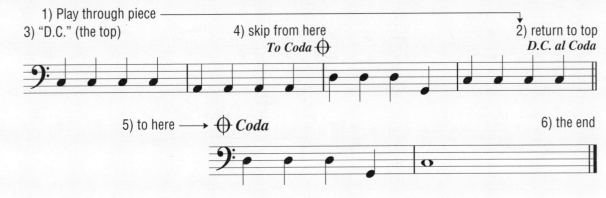

Pay attention to the form of this piece: 1) Take the repeat sign to the top, 2) play through to the second half of the song, 3) follow the D.C. al Coda back to the top, and, 4) at the coda sign, skip to the bottom of the page and play the coda measure.

CODA PENDANT

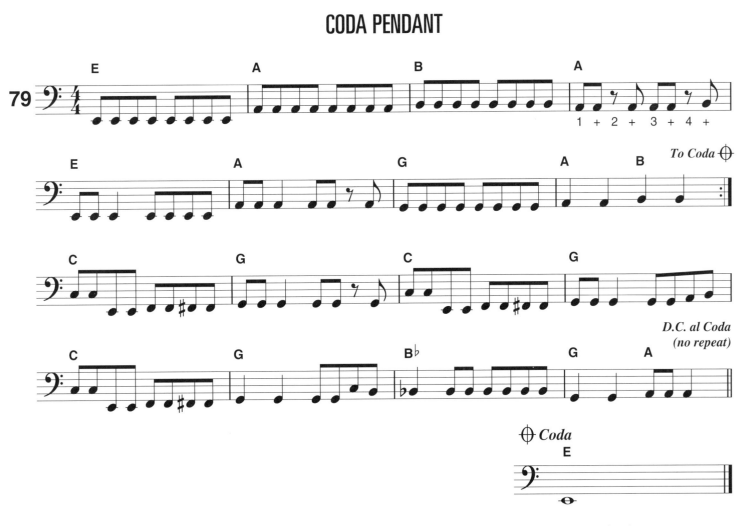

Staying on the root and "pumping out" eighth notes is a classic approach in rock bass playing. Pick style players may want to try the above song again, using all downstrokes (⊓). This option will give you a heavier sound than alternate picking (downstrokes and upstrokes) and is useful for some songs and styles.

The form of this piece is the same as the previous example, but now the first half of the song is called the A section, and the second half, the B section. These **rehearsal letters** make it easier to keep your place in longer songs and are a handy reference point when talking to other musicians.

DEE DEE

This 3/4 example uses ties within the measure.

USING A METRONOME

An important aspect of bass playing is keeping a steady tempo. A **metronome** will help you do this. Use an electronic or battery-powered model. First, learn an exercise slowly, and make sure you can play it correctly. Then, use a metronome to develop your tempo.

- Set your metronome to a slow tempo—50 beats per minute (bpm), for example.
- Let the click become the quarter-note pulse. Count along with it, "1, 2, 3..."
- Look at the exercise without the bass, and practice reading along with the click (e.g., "G, A, B...").
- Pick up your bass and read through the exercise with the click. Do your best to stay with the tempo.
- As you get more comfortable with the click, gradually speed up the tempo.

THE CLASSIC RHYTHM

The **dotted quarter/eighth note** combination (the "classic rhythm") is one of the most common in bass playing. Remember, a dot adds one half the value of whatever note it sits next to. A *dotted quarter note* equals the value of three eighth notes ($\bullet = \bullet + \bullet$). The classic rhythm is commonly used in one of two variations, and can be applied to many styles of music.

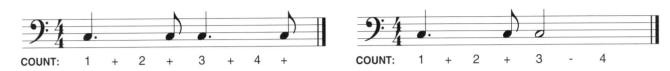

Practice the rhythm slowly, and count out loud. Once familiar with it, use a metronome clicking quarter notes.

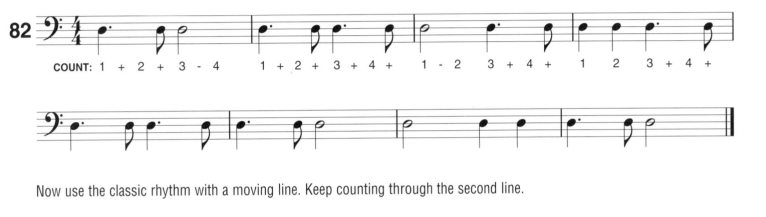

Now use the classic rhythm with a moving line. Keep counting through the second line.

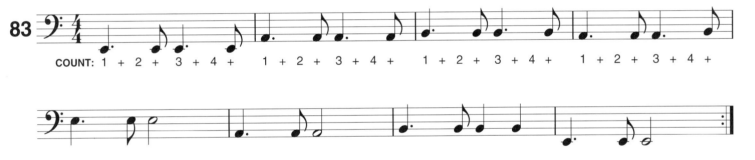

Now we start to add occasional eighth notes to the line. They add interest but keep the feel consistent.

DOWN HOME

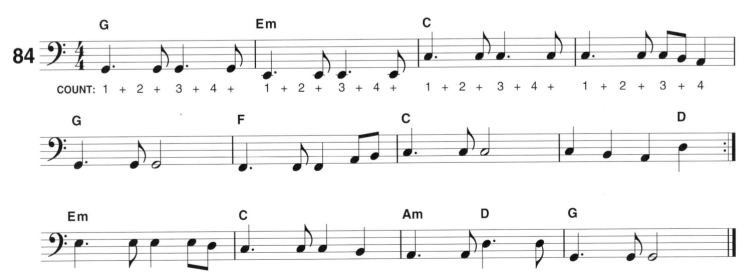

This one uses the classic rhythm in a bluesy, R&B style.

RAITT ON

Playing the classic rhythm with octaves is tricky at first. Practice your string crossing. Notice how the 1st ending line leads back to the top, and the 2nd ending line leads to the B section. Make sure to follow the form correctly.

MINOR'S TALE

A CLASSIC VARIATION

Sometimes the classic rhythm is played short: a quarter note followed by an eighth rest, with an eighth note on the up-beat. The space from the rest leaves room for the snare drum to hit on beats 2 and 4, giving the music a tight feel. To create the rest, simply mute the quarter note—either by lifting off the note with the left hand, or placing your plucking finger on the string.

When you get comfortable with this, use the metronome with a quarter-note click. Listen for the space left by the rest.

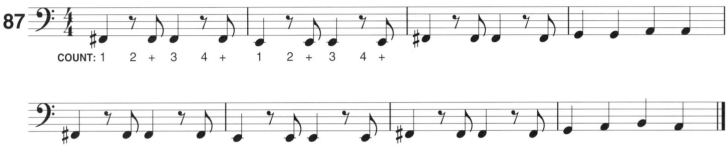

Here is a blues with the shortened classic rhythm.

CLASSIC BLUES

PETTY THIEF

THIRD POSITION

ON THE G STRING

Place your first finger at the 3rd fret. This is **3rd position**. On the G string, this introduces one new note, high C at the 5th fret.

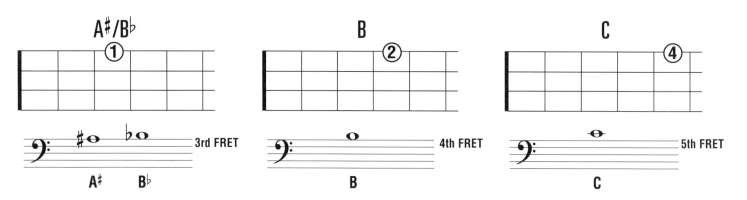

These are all the notes in 3rd position on the G string, starting with the high C.

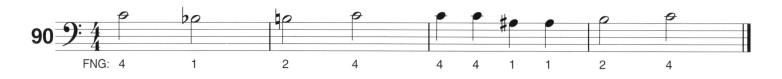

This example uses the open G string. Do not shift; keep the hand in 3rd position, and simply play the open string.

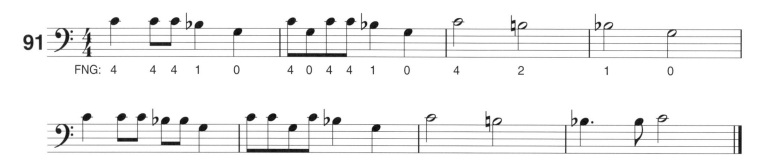

If you're playing in 1st or 2nd position, it will be necessary to shift up to the high C. Shifts are indicated with "–".

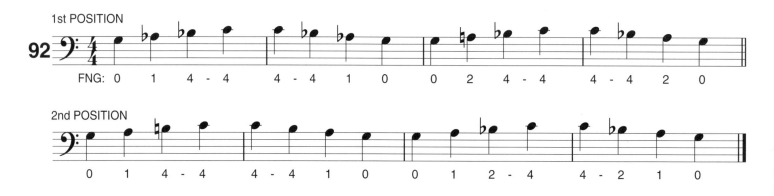

ON THE D STRING

Here are the notes on the D string in 3rd position. Notice that G at the 5th fret is the same note as the open G string.

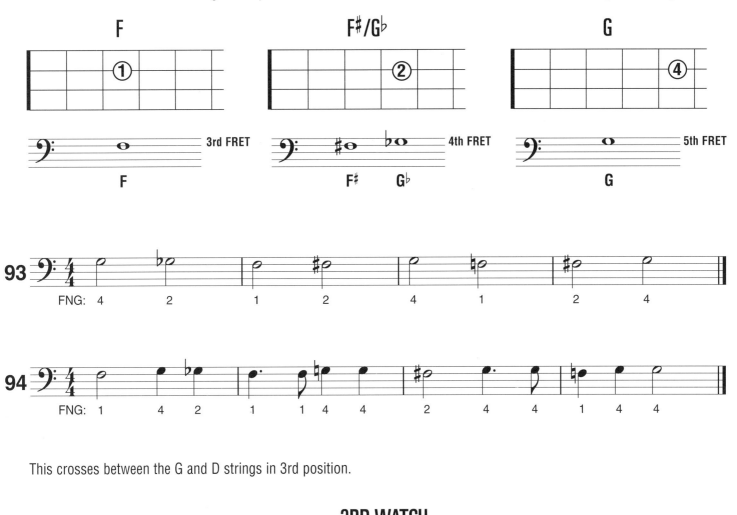

This crosses between the G and D strings in 3rd position.

ON THE A STRING

Here are the notes on the A string in 3rd position. The 5th fret is D, the same note as the open D string.

NEW OCTAVE: In 3rd position, we can play an octave on C.

FLYING LEAP

ON THE E STRING

Here are the notes on the E string in 3rd position. The 5th fret is A, the same note as the open A string.

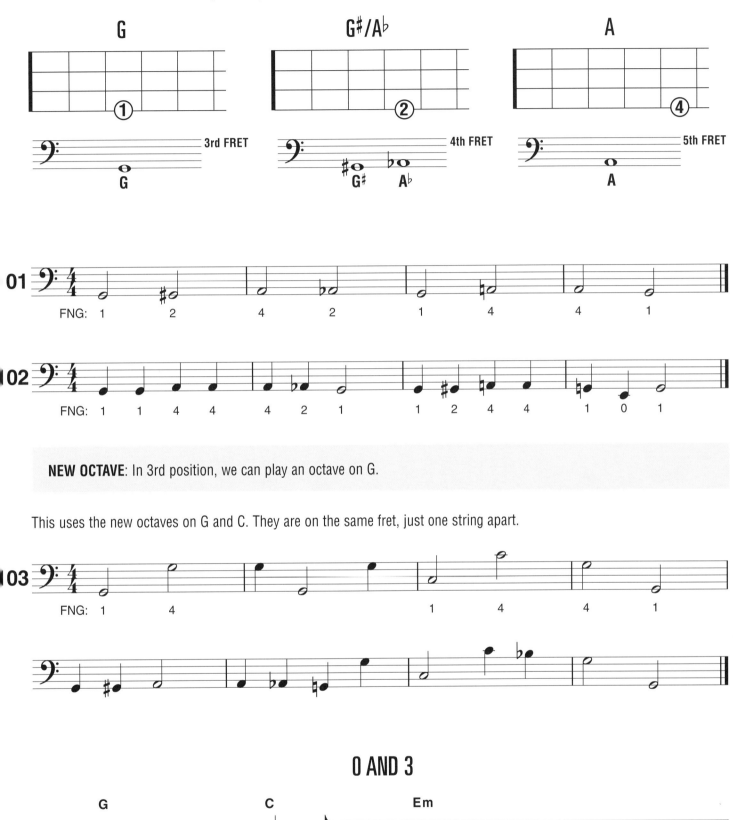

NEW OCTAVE: In 3rd position, we can play an octave on G.

This uses the new octaves on G and C. They are on the same fret, just one string apart.

0 AND 3

SHIFTING THROUGH THE POSITIONS

It is not uncommon to play a song in all three positions. Sometimes you have to shift the octave shape up and down.

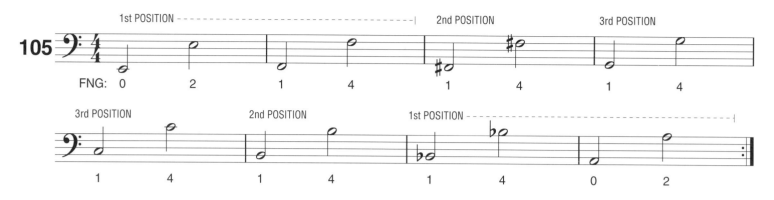

Sometimes it's better to shift to 3rd position for the sake of keeping groups of notes together on the fingerboard.

SHIFTY

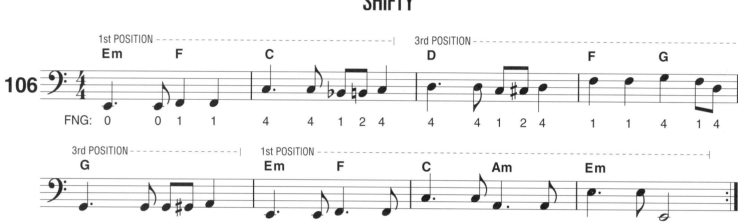

This jazz line shifts freely between 1st, 2nd, and 3rd positions. Brackets indicate what notes are in the same position. The shifts come after an open string, giving you a chance to change positions. Shift marks are placed in the fingering numbers.

SHIFT-CRAZY BLUES

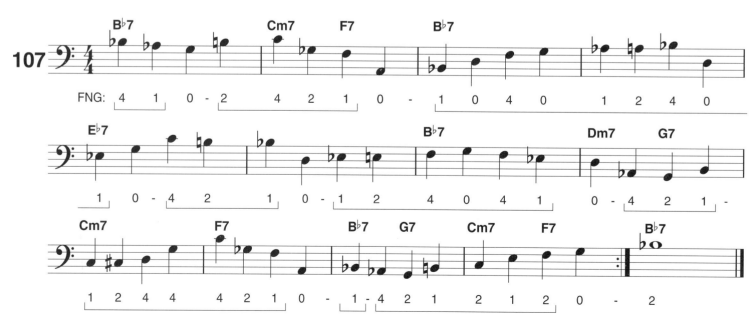

These examples change positions a few times. See if you can find the best way to play them on your own.

STONES-Y

ETUDE BRUTÉ

THE BOX SHAPE

The **box shape** is a common four-note pattern found in all styles of bass playing. It forms a square shape on the fingerboard that can be easily moved. The lowest note in the pattern is the root, and the highest note is the octave.

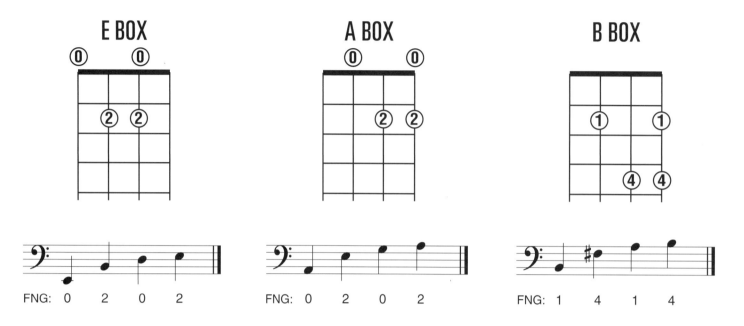

For octave jumps off the E string, place the right-hand thumb on the E string while playing the higher notes on the D string. Use the left hand to mute the open D string in measure 3.

For octave jumps off the A string, rest the right thumb on the A string and lean it against the E string while playing the higher notes on the G string. Use the left hand to mute the open G string in measure 3.

The B box has no open strings—so the fingering can be moved around the fingerboard easily. More on that soon.

E, A & B BOX

BOX LUNCH

BOX-E BLUES

MOVABLE BOXES

Movable boxes all have the same fingering. Place your 1st finger on any note on the E or A string; that becomes the root. The box shape for that root follows the fingering pattern shown below. Movable box patterns can be used to create your own bass lines.

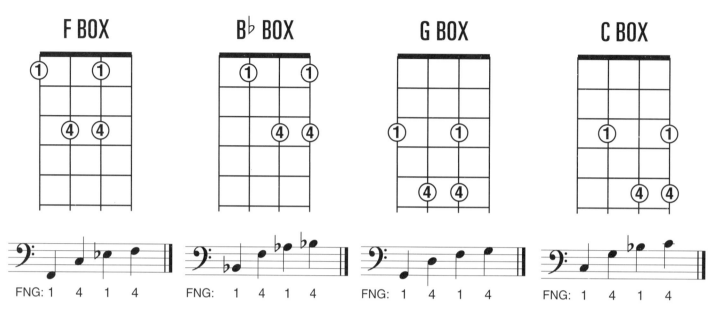

Remember to keep your left hand relaxed as you play. If these shapes feel like a stretch, let your hand pivot naturally at the thumb when moving between lower and higher notes.

The following examples show a one-measure box pattern. When you've learned the pattern thoroughly, play through the example by moving the pattern to the correct root, as indicated by the chord symbol above each measure.

YOUR MOVE

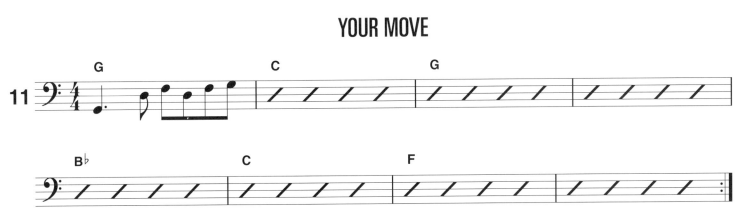

To play the F# box shape in this example, move your hand down to the 2nd fret.

MOVE IT

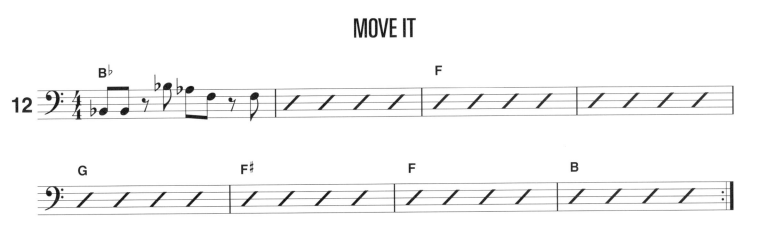

While the pattern remains the same, the A and E chords use the open E and A strings for their roots. Pay attention to muting your open strings.

MOVIE STAR

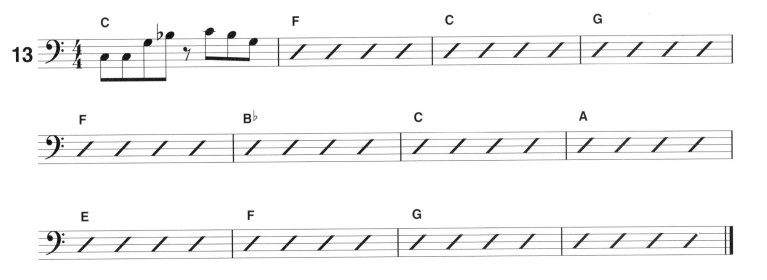

5TH POSITION

So far, we've played in 1st, 2nd, and 3rd positions. Let's continue to expand our knowledge of the fingerboard; playing in 5th position will give us access to a few new notes as well as alternate fingerings for notes we've already learned.

ON THE G STRING

Place your first finger on the 5th fret of the G string. We are still using the 1-2-4 fingering system.

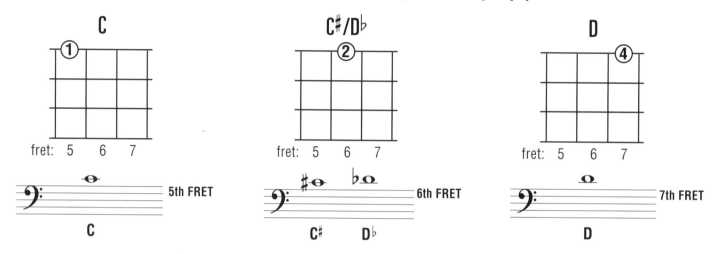

To get more comfortable with the notes in this position, say them aloud as you play: "C, C#, D…"

This example uses the open G string—keep the hand in 5th position and play the open string.

SHIFT PRACTICE

Many bass lines require you to play in several positions. It's important to be comfortable shifting between positions. Release the finger pressure before making the shift, and land on the new note as gently as possible.

Practice the shifts in example A individually, back and forth. Make the shifts as smooth as possible. Example B shifts from 5th position down to the open G, and back up.

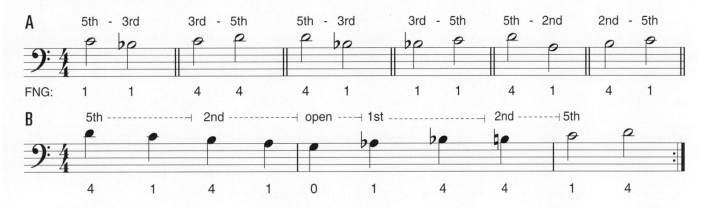

This example shifts between 3rd and 5th position.

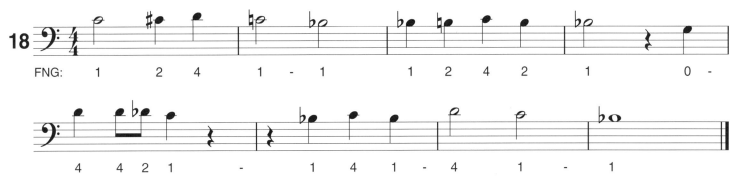

This example has many shifts. The important fingerings are marked, and all shifts are indicated by the "-" symbol.

SHIFTY HENRY

ON THE D STRING

Here are the notes in 5th position on the D string.

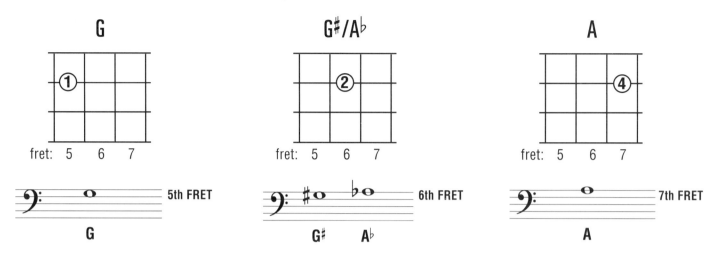

You'll recall these notes can also be found on the G string (open, 1st fret, and 2nd fret). Which position you choose to play them in will depend on the notes occurring before and after. For now, they'll be read in 5th position.

This example uses the open D string; stay in 5th position.

This example starts on open D, but it is still played in 5th position.

DEE GEE

58

Now practice playing across the D and G strings in 5th position.

This one crosses the D and G strings and "bounces" down to open D. Remember, it's all in 5th position.

Play on the D and G strings and shift between 5th, 3rd, and 1st positions. Remember: 3/4 time means 3 beats per bar.

5-3-1

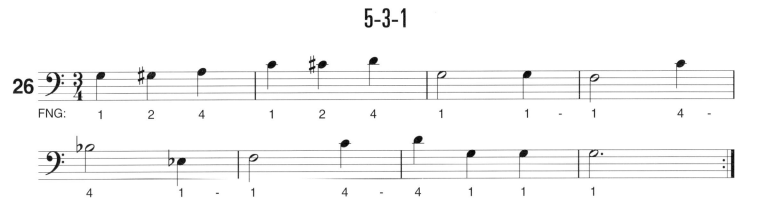

DIG IT

ON THE A STRING

Here are the notes on the A string in 5th position. These notes are also available on the D string: open, 1st fret, and 2nd fret. For now, we'll stick to 5th position locations.

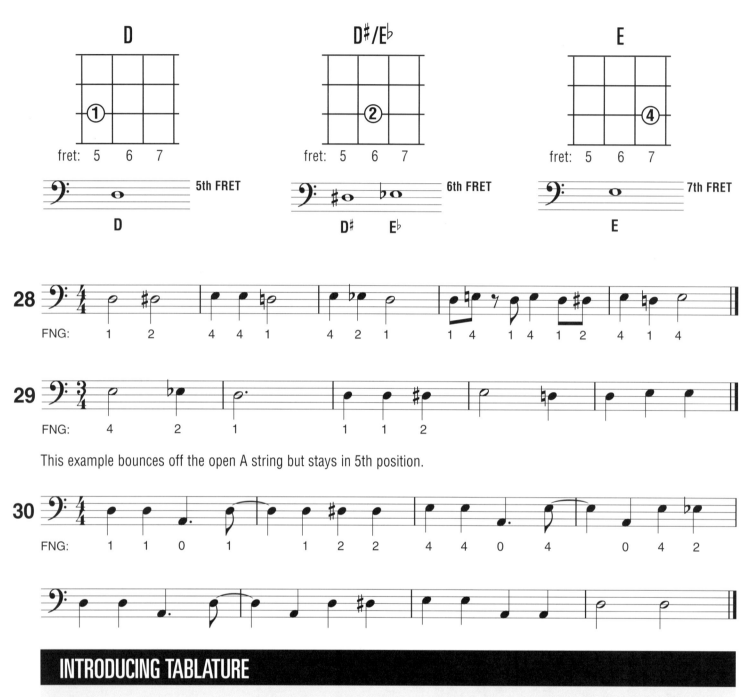

This example bounces off the open A string but stays in 5th position.

INTRODUCING TABLATURE

Tablature is a system of notating the specific location of notes on the fingerboard. In 5th position, there are many notes that could be played elsewhere on the neck; tablature (or "tab") is a handy way to indicate where they are best played.

The tab staff is 4 lines: the bottom line represents the E string; the next line is the A string, then the D string, and then the G string. Numbers on the lines represent frets. For each note on the staff, there will be a number in tab indicating the exact fret location of that note.

This example uses tablature to clearly indicate where the notes are played.

TAB HUNTER

This crosses the A, D, and G strings, and shifts between 5th and 3rd positions. Tablature makes it clear.

PAY THE TAB

ON THE E STRING

Here are the notes on the E string in 5th position. These notes are also found on the A string: open, 1st fret, and 2nd fret. These examples use 5th position.

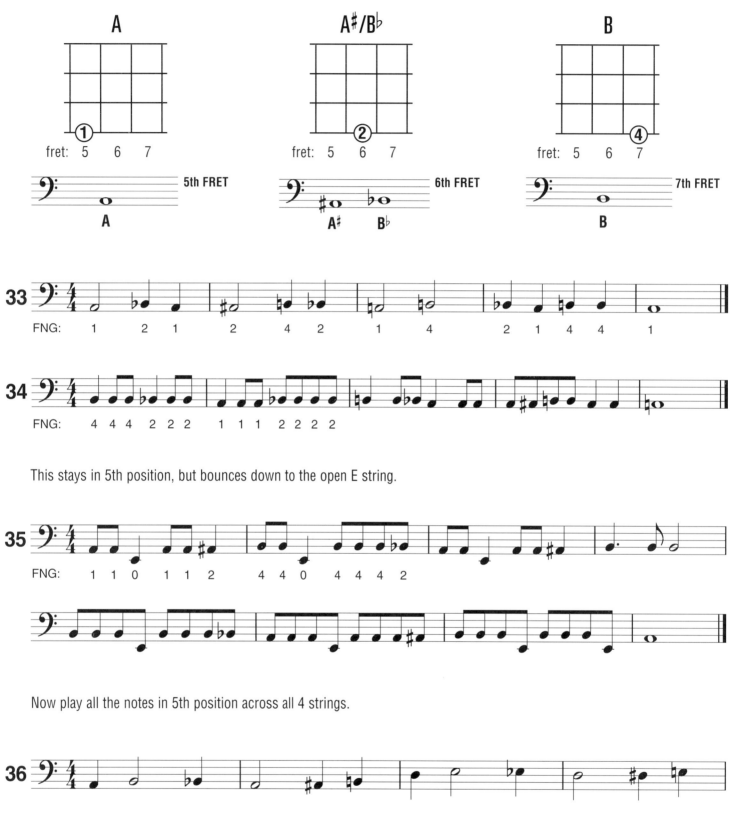

This stays in 5th position, but bounces down to the open E string.

Now play all the notes in 5th position across all 4 strings.

Crossing all four strings in 5th position, this one has some unusual switches between the open strings and their fretted counterparts. Check the tab carefully.

OPEN/CLOSED

DA BLUES

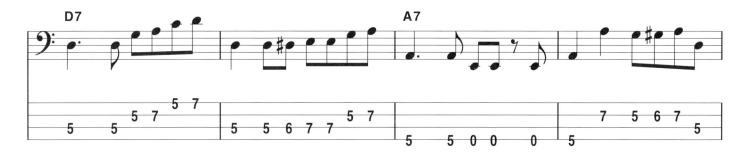

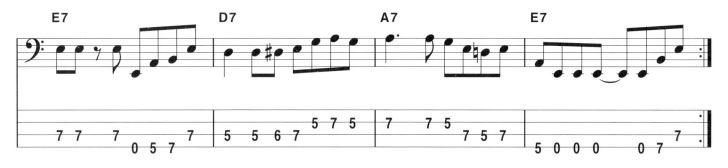

Here is a tune that shifts between several positions and crosses all four strings. Follow the tab, and experiment with different fingerings. Once you've got the fingerings down for this piece, practice reading it without looking at the tab. You'll develop a better sense of what you're playing and you'll keep up your note-reading "chops."

ALL TOGETHER NOW

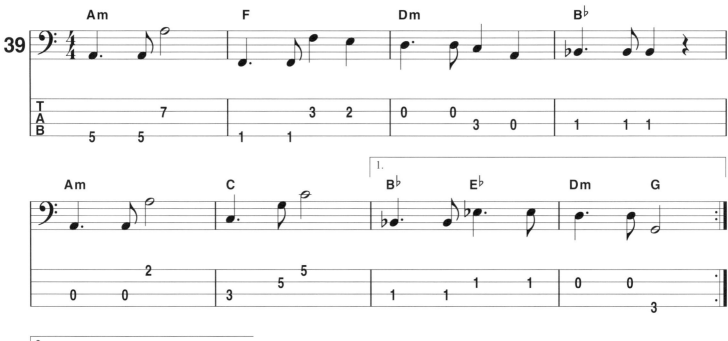

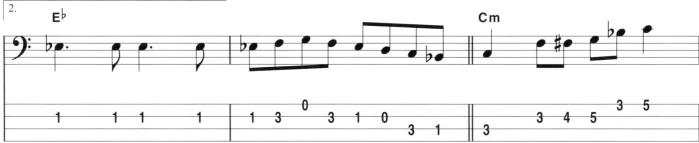

This is an example of a **walking bass** line. The constant quarter-note rhythm and non-repetitive note choices give it a distinct jazz flavor. This piece starts in 1st position, shifts up to 5th, and then shifts back down to 1st. Open strings are used to make the shifts easier. Try reading it first without looking at the tab, and see how well you do.

SWING TIME

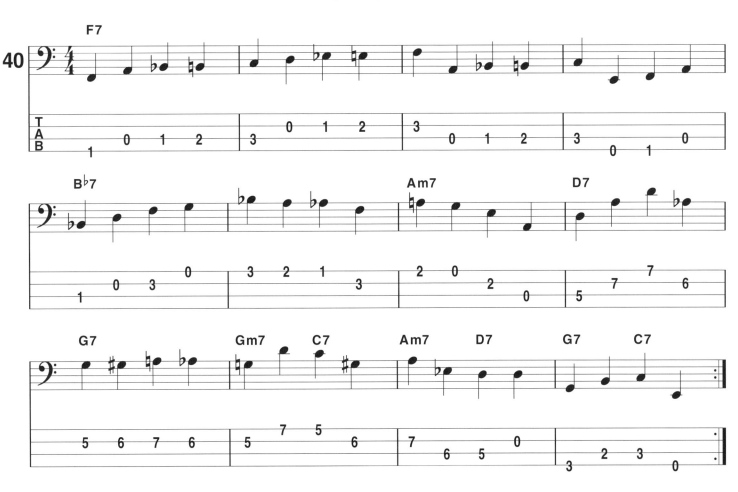

ONE FINGER PER FRET

Another fingering system commonly used on the bass assigns one finger to each fret. This expands what is available under your hand by one more note. This system is *not* advisable for box shapes as it puts too much strain on the hand. To use OFPF without strain, you must learn to use the **pivot** in the left hand between the 2nd and 3rd finger. Play a note with the 1st finger, then lay down the 2nd finger. When moving to the 3rd finger, release the 1st finger and pivot slightly on the 2nd finger and thumb to reach the note with the 3rd finger. Lay down the 4th finger next. Pivoting like this eliminates the need to stretch the hand open to reach the notes. Extended periods of stretching open your hand can be painful and potentially damaging. Stay relaxed and flexible as much as possible.

Practice playing across all four strings with OFPF. When you've reached the last note, reverse directions and come back down.

FNG: 1   2 ∧ 3   4   1   2 ∧ 3   4   1   2 ∧ 3   4   1   2 ∧ 3   4
          pivot   pivot   pivot   pivot

THE MAJOR SCALE

The **major scale** is a group of 8 notes that occur in a specific order. It is the basis of most popular music and is an important tool in developing an understanding of how music is structured.

The major scale is constructed by combining *whole steps* (the distance between 2 frets) and *half steps* (1 fret) in this pattern:

C MAJOR SCALE

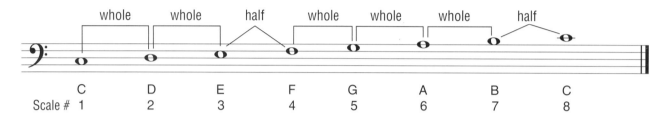

Each note in the scale is numbered 1 through 8. The 1st (and 8th) note is called the root or tonic (in this case, C). It is the note that gives the scale its name or **key**, and sounds like "home base." The numerical system is used to describe melodies, root motion, and many other musical elements.

Using the OFPF system and starting on the 2nd finger, the major scale falls naturally under the hand in one position. This is the "**universal fingering**" for the major scale; it will produce the scale in any key starting from the 2nd fret and above on the E or A strings. Here it is in C major.

major scale

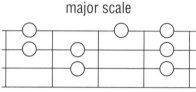

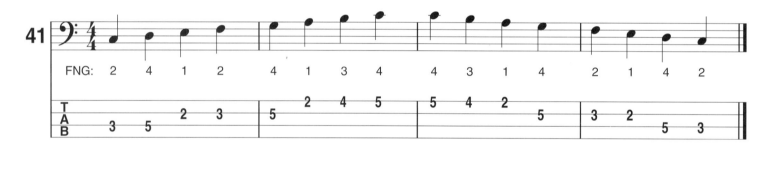

66

Remember: When using the OFPF system to play notes in a single position like this, allow your left hand to pivot naturally between the 2nd and 3rd fingers; always keep the hand relaxed.

The next two examples use the number system exclusively. Using the universal fingering in the key of C position, play the notes that correspond to the scale numbers. Say the scale numbers aloud. Pay attention to the note names as well.

SCALE SEQUENCE #1

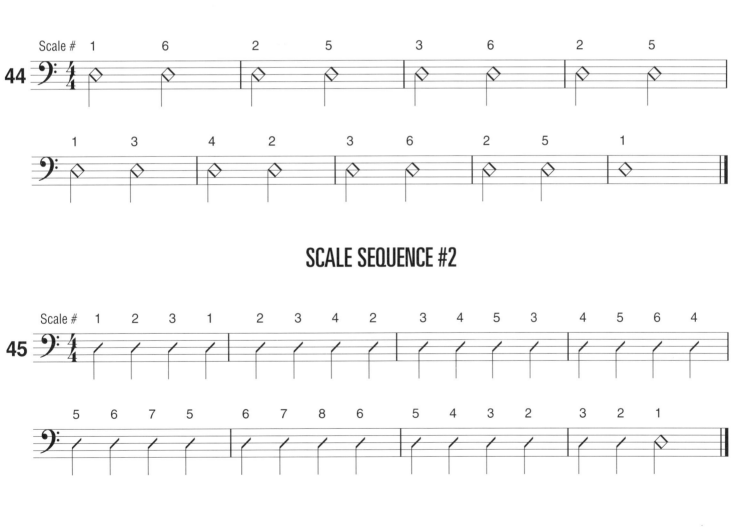

SCALE SEQUENCE #2

KEY SIGNATURES

If you examine the notes in the key of C, you'll notice that there are no sharps or flats. The half steps in the scale (between 3 & 4 and 7 & 8) naturally occur between E & F and B & C. In different keys, it is necessary to add sharps or flats to maintain the sequence of whole and half steps that produce the major scale.

Each new key has its own unique **key signature** that indicates which notes are sharp or flat. It appears at the beginning of a line of music. Here are the key signatures for keys up to 5 sharps and 5 flats.

SHARP KEYS

G MAJOR   D MAJOR   A MAJOR   E MAJOR   B MAJOR

FLAT KEYS

F MAJOR   B♭ MAJOR   E♭ MAJOR   A♭ MAJOR   D♭ MAJOR

Sharps or flats indicated in the key signature are played automatically unless cancelled out by a natural sign (♮).

To get familiar with the above keys, play them first in **open position**—that is, starting on the lowest possible root on the fingerboard, and using as many open strings as possible. Some of these keys/scales will be easier to play this way than others. The keys of G, A, E, F, and B♭ will be especially useful. Use the 1-2-4 fingering system, and refer to the fingerings and shifts as needed.

Play each scale several times, and be sure to watch for sharps and flats. Say the note names as you play.

In 2nd position.

G MAJOR

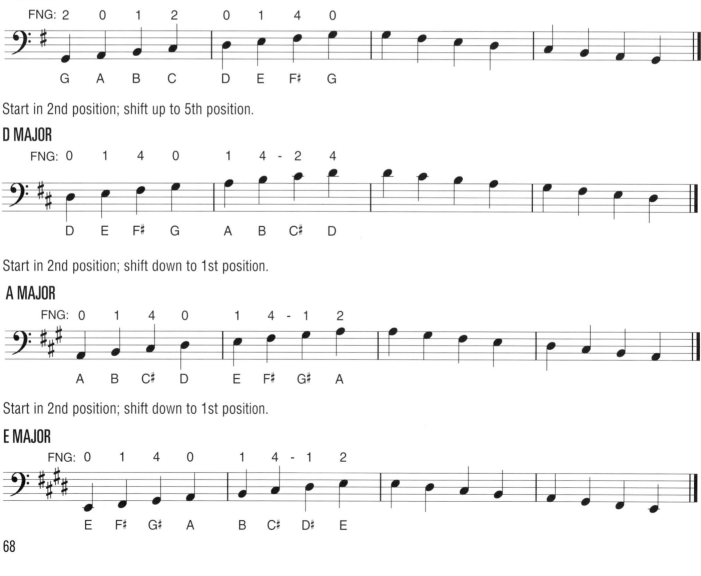

Start in 2nd position; shift up to 5th position.

D MAJOR

Start in 2nd position; shift down to 1st position.

A MAJOR

Start in 2nd position; shift down to 1st position.

E MAJOR

Try the OPFP system for this one. (Start on the 2nd fret, A string.)

B MAJOR

In 1st position.

F MAJOR

In 1st position.

B♭ MAJOR

Start in 1st position; shift up to 5th (with a stretch).

E♭ MAJOR

In 1st position. (Use OFPF at the start.)

A♭ MAJOR

Start in 1st position, then shift up. (Again, try OFPF at the start.)

D♭ MAJOR

TIP: Before playing any piece of music, check the key signature. Play the corresponding scale up and down, saying the note names aloud. You'll be warmed up and ready to play!

UNIVERSAL FINGERINGS

Of course, all the major keys can also be played with the universal fingering (2-4, 1-2-4, 1-3-4). E, B, F, and E♭ are in higher positions than you've learned, but it's simple to plug in the fingering and play the scale.

Again, play each scale several times. First say the note names, then the scale numbers.

Start on the 3rd fret, E string.

G MAJOR

FNG: 2   4   1   2   4   1   3   4

G   A   B   C   D   E   F#   G
Scale #   1   2   3   4   5   6   7   8

Start on the 5th fret, A string.

D MAJOR

D   E   F#   G   A   B   C#   D

Start on the 5th fret, E string.

A MAJOR

A   B   C#   D   E   F#   G#   A

Start on the 7th fret, A string.

E MAJOR

E   F#   G#   A   B   C#   D#   E

Start on the 7th fret, E string.

B MAJOR

B   C#   D#   E   F#   G#   A#   B

Start on the 8th fret, A string.

F MAJOR

F   G   A   B♭   C   D   E   F

Start on the 6th fret fret, E string.

B♭ MAJOR

B♭   C   D   E♭   F   G   A   B♭

Start on the 6th fret, A string.

E♭ MAJOR

E♭   F   G   A♭   B♭   C   D   E♭

Start on the 4th fret, E string.

A♭ MAJOR

A♭   B♭   C   D♭   E♭   F   G   A♭

Start on the 4th fret, A string.

D♭ MAJOR

D♭   E♭   F   G♭   A♭   B♭   C   D♭

Once you are comfortable with each scale in its various positions, play them all using these numerical sequences. For more practice in this area, go back to Scale Sequences #1 and #2 and play them in all keys.

SCALE SEQUENCE #3

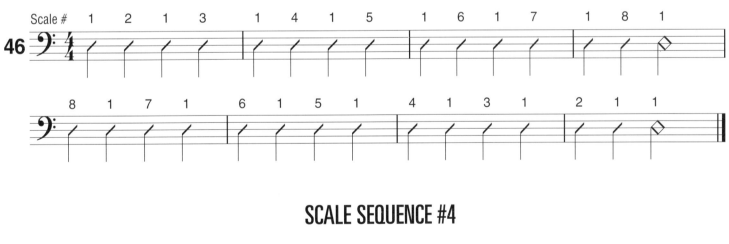

Scale #   1   2   1   3   1   4   1   5   1   6   1   7   1   8   1

8   1   7   1   6   1   5   1   4   1   3   1   2   1   1

SCALE SEQUENCE #4

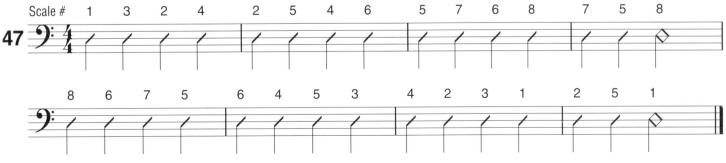

Scale #   1   3   2   4   2   5   4   6   5   7   6   8   7   5   8

8   6   7   5   6   4   5   3   4   2   3   1   2   5   1

Now it's time to play. Check the key signature, and play the sharps and flats as indicated. Find your own fingerings.

PASTA MON

While the notes in this next piece go below the root D, it is still playable in the D major scale position at the 5th fret. You could consider this a "lower extension" of the universal fingering. The piece can also be played in open position.

major scale
(w/lower extension)

D-LISH

Try this in the universal scale fingering; you can also read it in open position.

A-FLAT TIRE

OPEN E

This can be played in open G and universal positions. Try them both.

G3

This, too, can be played in open and universal positions.

B-FLAT JUMP

THE CLASSIC BLUES LINE

This very familiar bass line follows a pattern that fits right into the universal scale fingering, making it very easy to play in any key. Hint: You'll need an upper extension for the C7 and D7 chords. (Refer to the diagram below.)

In this key, the line can also be played in open position; try it both ways.

GEE BLUES

This line has variations in the main pattern and in measures 9 through 12. They are interchangeable with the original line. The key of A can also be played in open position, but measures 9 and 10 need to be repositioned. Can you figure out how to do it?

AAY, BLUES!

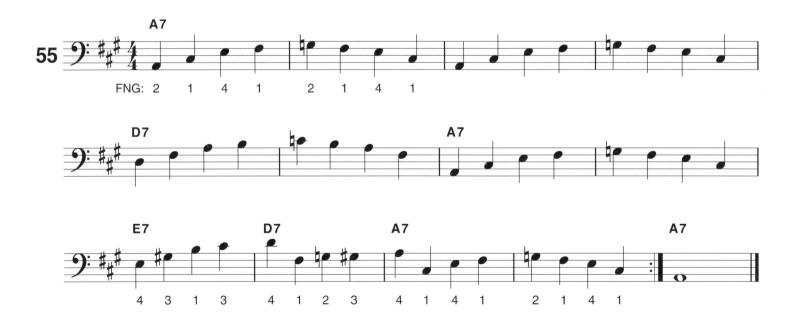

E is a very popular key for the blues. Shifting the classic line into E requires you to play in open position. This version is a "doubled up" rhythm using eighth notes. This has a more "rock 'n' roll" feel to it, but the line is the same as the original.

LOW DOWN

UNDERSTANDING BASS LINES

An effective way to understand bass lines is to determine the scale numbers that represent the notes. By now you can figure out the scale numbers within a key, but when chords change, you'll sometimes find it easier to think of the notes in relationship to the new chord. The root of each new chord becomes scale number 1. In the example below, the scale numbers on the E7 chord are 1-3-5-6-8-5-3. When it moves to the A7 chord, the A (the root) becomes the new number 1, so the pattern for the A7 chord is also 1-3-5-6-8-6-5-3.

Rather than figure out the numbers for the entire line in the key of E, each new chord represents a separate "key"—not literally, but in terms of playing and understanding the line. This approach can be especially effective in playing blues.

SYNCOPATED EIGHTH NOTES

Syncopation is the placement of rhythmic accents on weak beats or weak portions of beats. Syncopated eighth notes, for example, emphasize the upbeat, or "and" of a beat. They are an important part of rock, blues, funk, R&B, soul, latin, jazz, and even country music.

Practice these slowly, counting the eighth notes aloud "1 + 2 +" etc. In order for syncopation to sound correct, the downbeats need to be felt. Once you are comfortable with the rhythms, use a metronome clicking on quarter notes.

Fingerstyle players, remember to alternate between index (i) and middle (m) fingers. To mute the string during a rest, place the alternate finger down early—stopping the string's vibration—before playing the next note. Pick style players, continue to use downstrokes on downbeats, and upstrokes on upbeats (or play all downstrokes, if you prefer). Be sure to mute all rests with your left hand.

OFF BEAT

FUNKY SOUL GROOVE

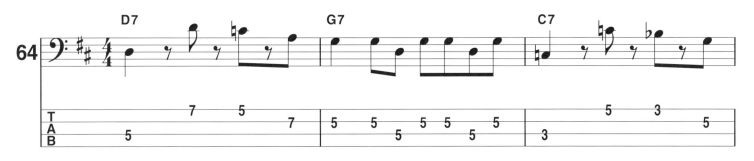

THAT '70S THING

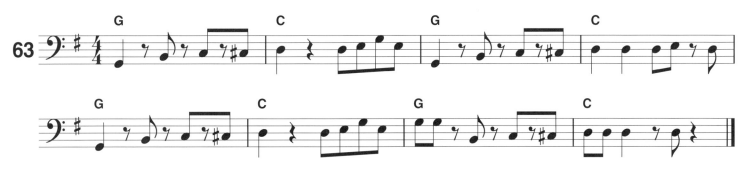

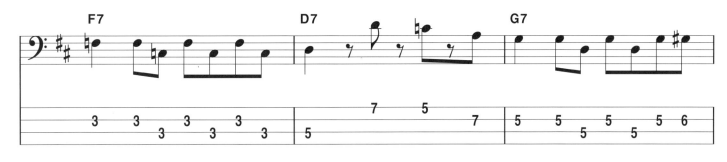

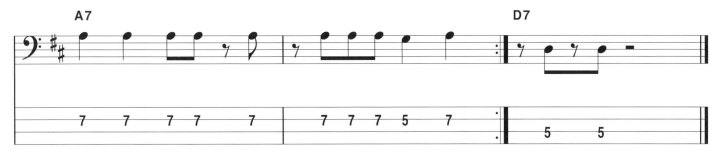

THE MAJOR TRIAD

A *major triad* is a three-note chord structure built with the root, 3rd, and 5th notes of the major scale.

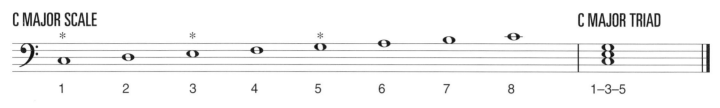

On instruments like guitar and piano, chords are typically played with all notes ringing at the same time. On bass, they are played in a melodic sequence, called an *arpeggio*. Arpeggios are used in bass lines to outline the chords of a song.

Major triads can be played in all keys within the universal scale position. The octave is added but isn't considered a new note as it is the same as the root.

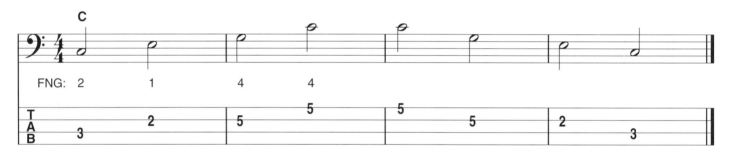

But they can also be played this way in any key: Don't try to stretch for the 3rd of the chord; shift up to the 4th finger.

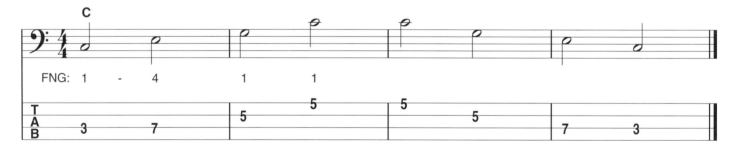

In many keys, open strings are also available.

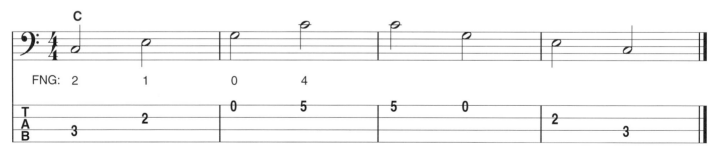

When deciding which fingering to use, consider which is most convenient to play, but also consider which sounds better.

Here are the *flat key* major triads with various fingerings. Practice them each way several times, say the note names, and the scale numbers. Once familiar, use a metronome clicking quarter notes.

F MAJOR

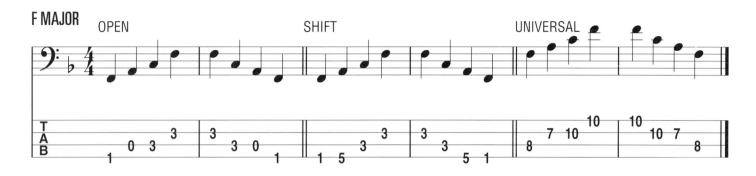

B♭ MAJOR

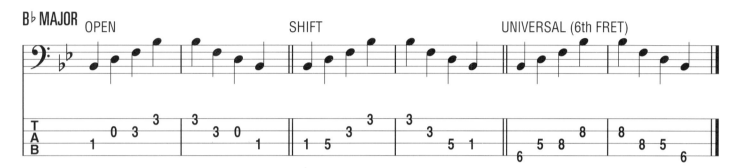

E♭ MAJOR

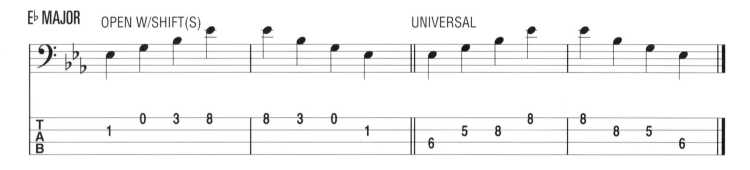

A♭ MAJOR

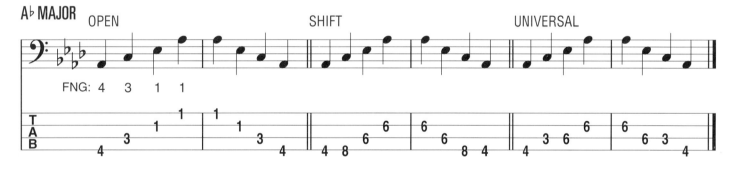

D♭ MAJOR

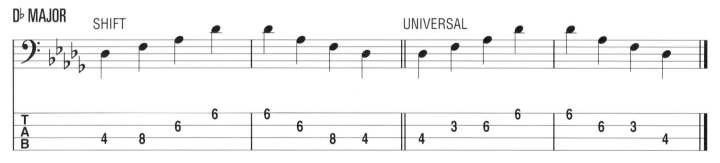

Here are the *sharp key* major triads in various fingerings. Practice them the same way.

G MAJOR

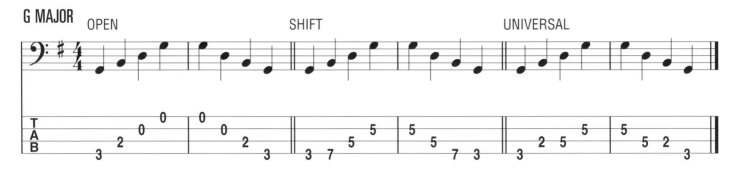

D MAJOR

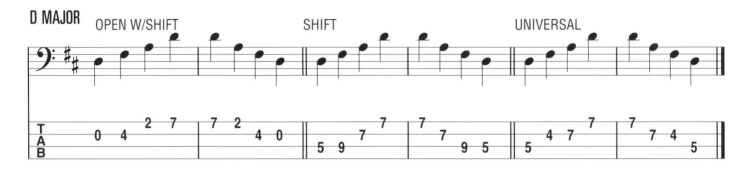

A MAJOR

E MAJOR

B MAJOR

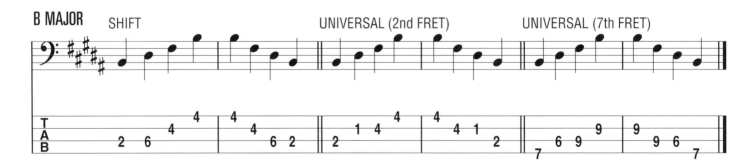

Triads are very effective for outlining a chord progression; they are a classic approach to constructing a bass line.

TRI AGAIN

Remember how D.C. al Coda and Coda signs work? In the piece above, take the repeat sign back to letter A; next time, go on to letter B. When you reach the D.C. al Coda indication, go back to the top of the song and play until the To Coda (⊕)indication. From there, skip to the Coda at the end of the song.

This example takes the basic triad and adds an additional note, the **6th**, for a slightly different type of line.

FUNKY LI'L BLUES

THE MINOR SCALE

The **minor scale** has a flatted 3rd scale degree, which gives it a "sadder" quality compared to major. While there are several types of minor scale, we'll learn what's called "natural minor." In addition to the flatted 3rd, it also has flatted 6th and 7th degrees.

C NATURAL MINOR

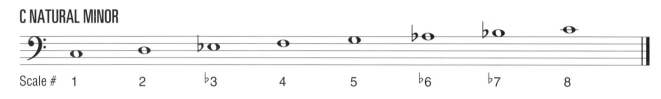

The natural minor scale also has a universal fingering that will work in any key. It uses the OFPF system and starts on the 1st finger.

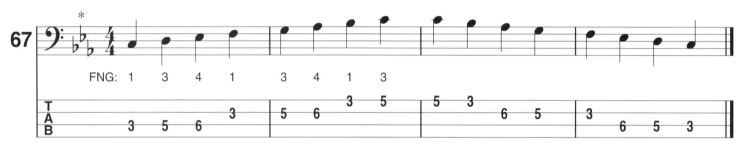

Practice the natural minor scale first saying the note names, then saying the scale numbers. Also practice it using this scale sequence.

MINOR SCALE SEQUENCE

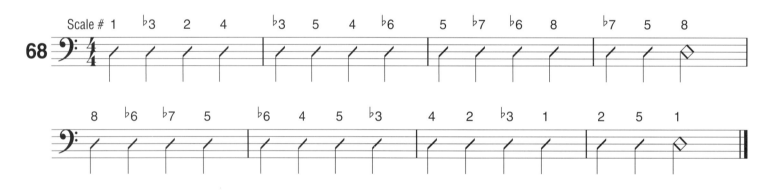

RELATIVE MINOR AND MAJOR

The natural minor scale and the major scale are related to one another. Play the C major scale; the 6th note is A. Now play A natural minor. It contains the same exact notes as C major. This is because A minor is the **relative minor** of C major. They share the same key signature.

To find the relative minor of any major key, count down to the 6th scale degree of that major scale. In reverse, to find the relative major of any minor key, count up to the flat 3rd of that minor scale.

*Understanding how the relative major/minor concept works, you now see that the proper key signature for C minor is actually the same as the key signature for Eb major: that is, three flats.

To get familiar with the natural minor keys, let's play them first in open position—where possible—and then in the universal natural minor fingering: 1-3-4, 1-3-4, 1-3. Say the note names as you play, and then the scale numbers.

First, here is A minor. Start on the open A string for open position; on the 5th fret, E string for universal fingering.

A MINOR

A   B   C   D   E   F   G   A

Now try the *flat key* natural minor scales.

Start on open D for open position; on the 5th fret, A string for universal.

D MINOR

D   E   F   G   A   B♭   C   D

Start on 3rd fret, E string for open position or universal.

G MINOR

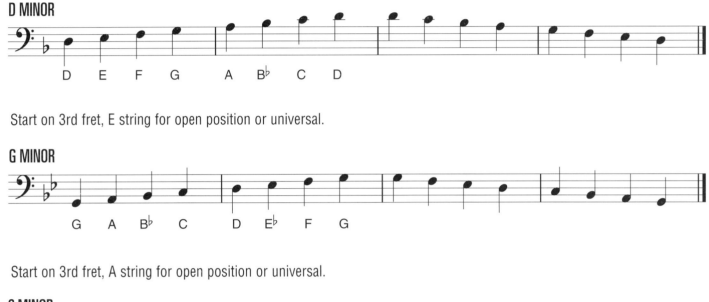

G   A   B♭   C   D   E♭   F   G

Start on 3rd fret, A string for open position or universal.

C MINOR

C   D   E♭   F   G   A♭   B♭   C

Start on 1st fret, E string for universal. Also try one octave higher, at the 8th fret, A string.

F MINOR

F   G   A♭   B♭   C   D♭   E♭   F

Start on 1st fret, A string or 6th fret, E string.

B♭ MINOR

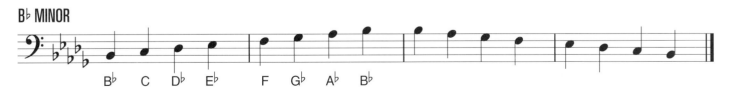

B♭   C   D♭   E♭   F   G♭   A♭   B♭

Here are the *sharp key* natural minor scales.

Start on open E for open position; at the 7th fret, A string for universal (one octave higher).

E MINOR

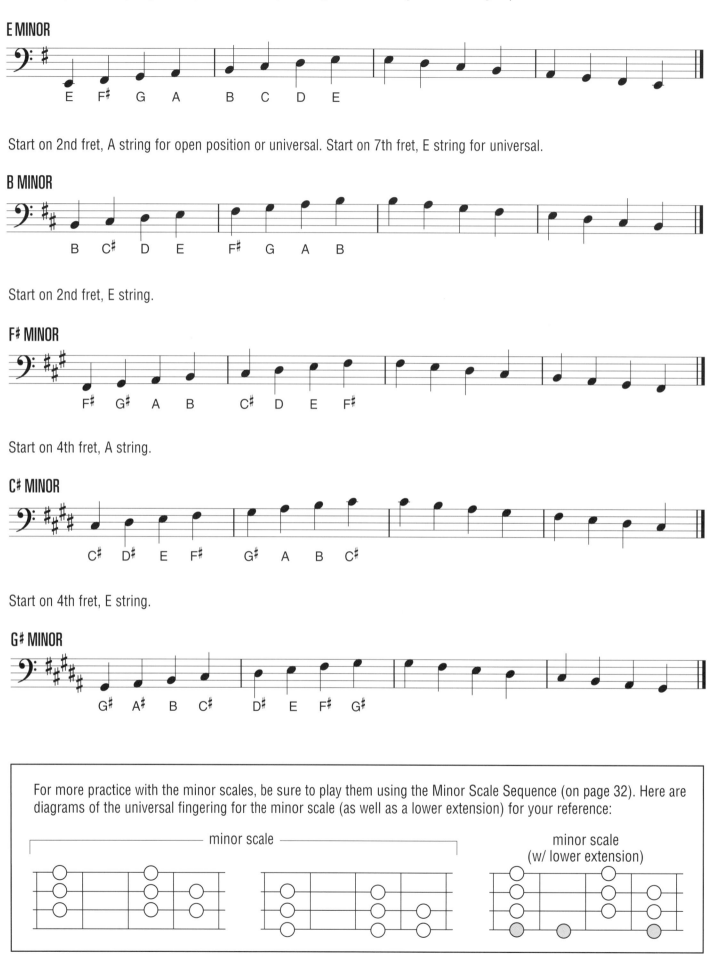

Start on 2nd fret, A string for open position or universal. Start on 7th fret, E string for universal.

B MINOR

Start on 2nd fret, E string.

F# MINOR

Start on 4th fret, A string.

C# MINOR

Start on 4th fret, E string.

G# MINOR

For more practice with the minor scales, be sure to play them using the Minor Scale Sequence (on page 32). Here are diagrams of the universal fingering for the minor scale (as well as a lower extension) for your reference:

minor scale

minor scale
(w/ lower extension)

Identify the keys below. Play the corresponding minor scale, in open or in universal position, saying the note names aloud. Then play the piece.

HOUSE O' HORROR

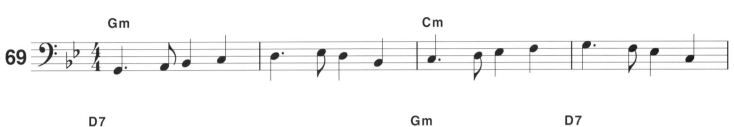

NOIR

JAZZ MINOR

MODULATION

When a piece of music changes key, it's called a **modulation**. The new key signature is displayed on the staff, and all the new accidentals for that key are in effect until another modulation occurs.

MINOR MODULATION

This scale exercise modulates every two measures. Keep careful track of the new accidentals as they appear.

MOD CRAZY

MINOR TRIADS

Minor triads are built from the minor scale using the root, flat 3rd, and 5th notes.

A MINOR SCALE   A MINOR TRIAD

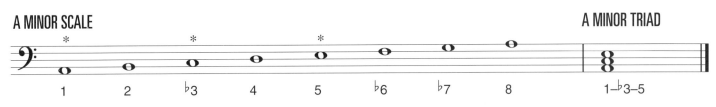

Minor triads also have a universal fingering that works in all keys. Again, we add the octave on top.

A MINOR
UNIVERSAL FINGERING

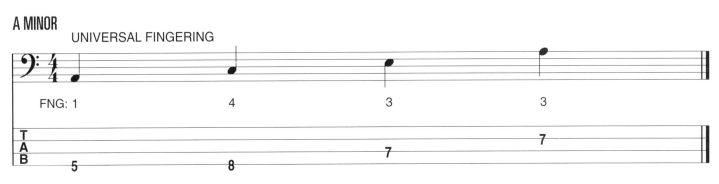

Many minor triads can also be played in open position.

A MINOR
OPEN POSITION

Another fingering that is a bit tricky spans across all four strings.

A MINOR
ACROSS 4 STRINGS

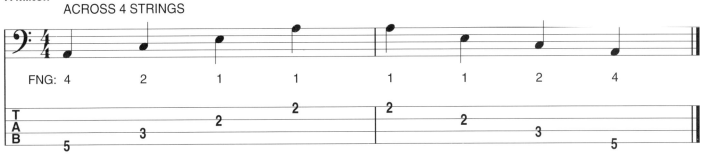

Here are the sharp key minor triads with various fingerings. Practice them each way several times, saying the note names and scale numbers. Once they are familiar, use a metronome clicking quarter notes.

E MINOR

B MINOR

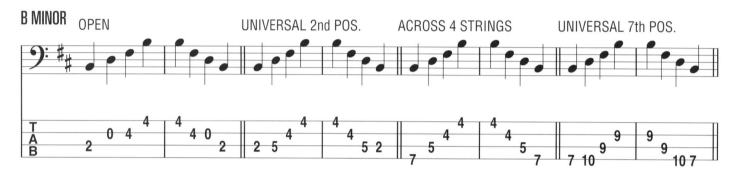

F# MINOR

C# MINOR

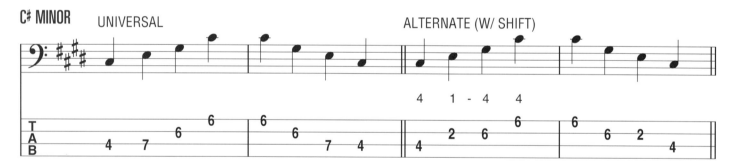

G# MINOR

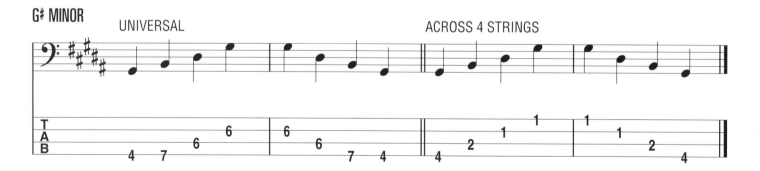

Here are the flat key minor triads.

D MINOR

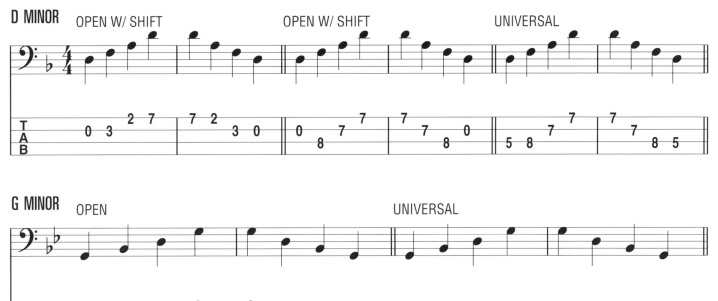

G MINOR

C MINOR

F MINOR

B♭ MINOR

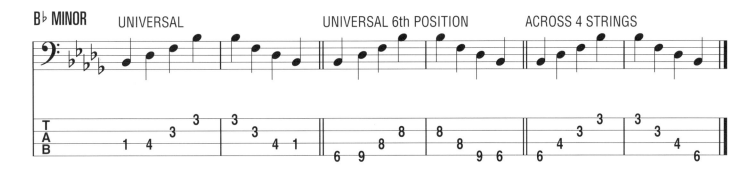

Use your knowledge of triads—both minor and major—to play through these next pieces.

BOGEY MAN

This reggae tune has a tricky modulation, from 5 sharps to 4 flats.

ROOTS

Often songs in minor keys will modulate to the relative major key. This has a swingy, old time jazz feel; give the eighth notes a bouncy feel.

GYPSY SWING

Of course, minor triads are not restricted to minor keys. This rhumba in G major includes several minor triads.

ROOM-BA WITH A VIEW

EIGHTH-NOTE TRIPLETS

Triplets manage to squeeze three notes into the space of one. For example, instead of dividing the quarter note in half as in regular eighth notes, it is split into thirds—resulting in eighth-note triplets.

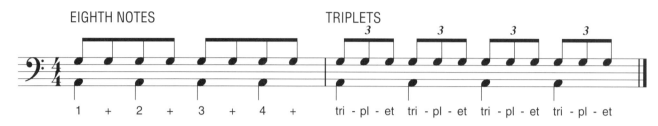

Evenly space the word "tri-pl-et" starting on each quarter note; make sure they feel relaxed and "round." In pick style playing, triplets can represent a real challenge. Be sure to keep downstrokes on downbeats (1, 2, 3, and 4). This means either playing all downstrokes, or using a downstroke-upstroke-downstroke combination.

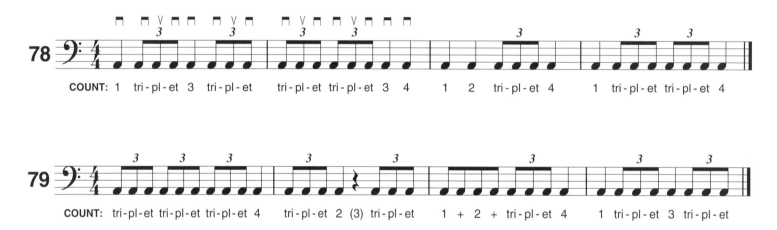

Triplets can also be written with a connecting bracket—for example, if there is a rest within the triplet. When an eighth-note rest is placed within the triplet bracket, it becomes an eighth-note triplet rest. The missing syllable is a place marker.

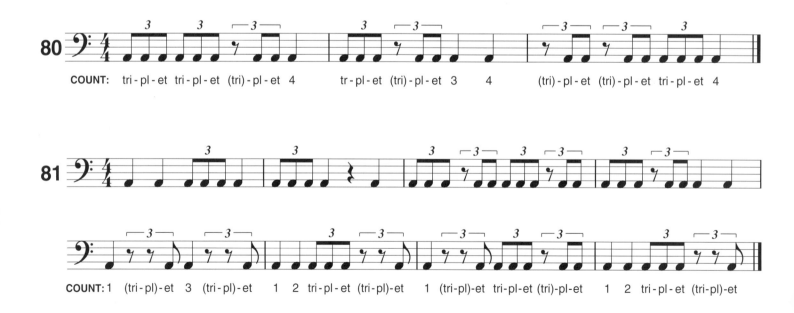

This bass line has a 12/8 feel.

THE '50S

12/8 TIME

Sometimes, triplet-based music is notated in **12/8 time**. In 12/8, there are twelve eighth notes in each measure. However, the dotted quarter note (♩.) gets the emphasis—so the feel is still essentially four beats per measure, with each beat divided into three eighth notes.

COUNT: 1 – 2 – 3   4   5   6   7 – 8 – 9   10   11   12

This movable box shape line takes advantage of the open D string to facilitate the position shift.

BUMPIN'

THE SHUFFLE RHYTHM

A popular rhythm based on eighth-note triplets is the **shuffle**. It is the foundation of most blues, as well as being used in many other styles. The shuffle uses the 1st and 3rd beats of an eighth-note triplet to create a familiar "stuttering" feel.

The shuffle can also be written and played with a longer, smoother feel. In this case, the first two beats of the eighth-note triplet are joined, adding up to a quarter note. Because triplets can be cumbersome to read, this feel is also sometimes notated simply as eighth notes, but with a shuffle indication ($\sqcap = \overset{3}{\sqcap}$) at the start of the piece.

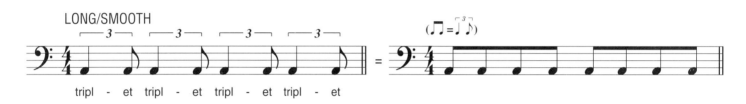

Here are some classic shuffle feels. This first one is of the "long/smooth" type.

OLD DAYS

94

The next example uses a notation shorthand called **one**- and **two-measure repeats**. They indicate to repeat either the previous one or two measures.

1 MEASURE REPEATS   2 MEASURE REPEAT

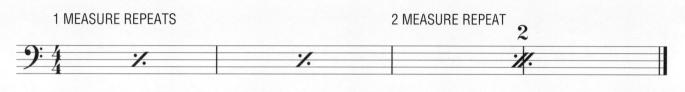

BAD BONE

Here is a box shape line that's been "shuffle-ized."

UPTOWN DOWN

Here's shuffle-ized version of the classic blues line in A. This variation has the flatted 7th scale degree instead of the octave for the top note.

CLASSIC FLAT 7

This tune has a gospel feel.

ROLLIN'

GO ON

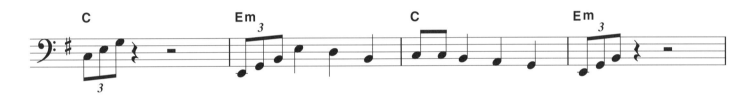

THE CHROMATIC WALKUP

The **walkup** is a classic pattern used in rock, R&B, gospel, funk, blues, and many other styles. It starts on the root of a chord and uses a chromatic (half-step) motion to return to the root.

The simplest version of this is a one-measure pattern that drops from the root to the 6th and then moves back up.

The walkup can also drop down to the 3rd of the lower octave for a longer buildup.

The following walkup moves up to the octave. To get back to the starting note, it drops to the 3rd and goes up to the 5th. It jumps down a 7th in the middle of the pattern to finish back at the root. Notice where the shift happens.

TIP: The pattern above is based on a universal fingering (one-finger-per-fret), so it's movable to any root, chord, or key. Try it on another root on the E or A string. (The shorter versions shown above are also movable.)

This extended version of the walkup alternates between low and high movement. It's a great way to keep the bass line interesting over a long section of one chord. Notice the shifts.

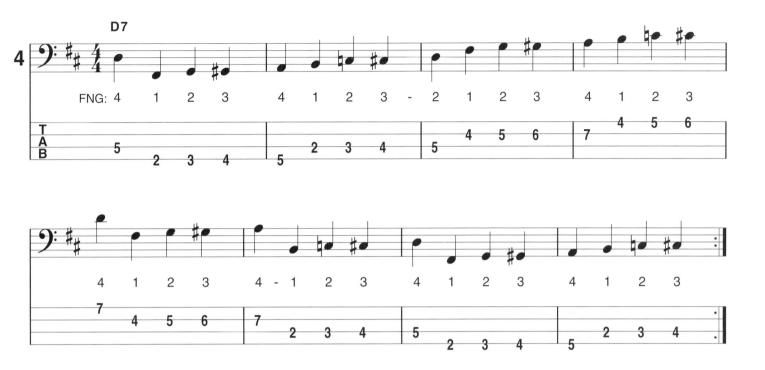

The walkup can be played in any key, but the fingering does change in open position. Also, notice how the line has been modified at the end to bring it back to the E chord.

OPEN UP

Playing your notes short is called **staccato**. The little spaces in between each note gives the bass line a "pumping" feel. Staccato is indicated by a small dot (•) above the note.

Here's how it's done: Play the first note with either the index (i) or middle (m) finger. Before playing the next note, place the alternate finger on the string and stop its vibration. Then play the next note. Practice this slowly first, then gradually increase the tempo.

If playing pick style, use your left hand to stop the string's vibration.

This classic variation on the chromatic walkup is known as the "double stroke." Make each note even and consistent. It's written staccato, but also experiment with different note lengths. Start on the 4th finger using the 1-2-4 fingering system, but switch to one-finger-per-fret (OFPF) in measure 3. When you repeat, use the 1st finger to play the low C.

DOUBLE UP

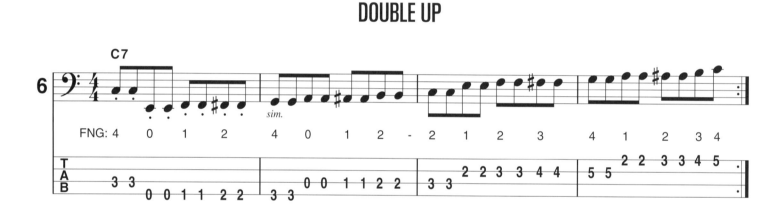

Here are two ways of notating a syncopated eighth-note rhythm. They sound identical, but the untied version is less confusing to the eye.

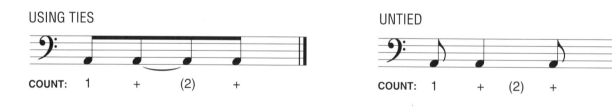

REZ - Q

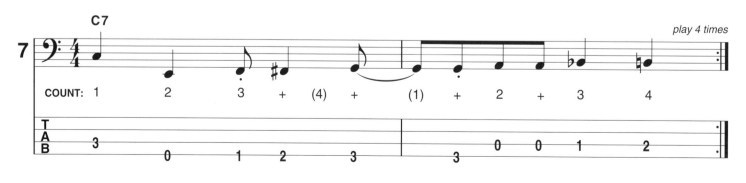

This moves the walkup through several chord changes. Slowly count your way through the extended syncopation in measures 6 and 7.

CURTIS

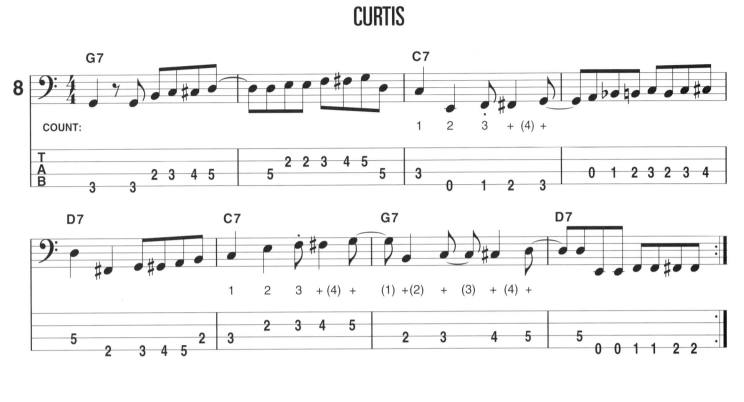

KICKIN' IT

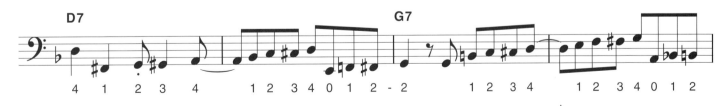

SIXTEENTH NOTES

Sixteenth notes break each quarter note into four equal subdivisions. They are counted, "1-ee-and-uh, 2-ee-and-uh," etc. In groups, sixteenth notes are written with a double beam connecting them. Separately, they have a double "flag."

COUNT: 1 e + a 2 e + a 3 e + a 4 e + a

Practice sixteenths slowly, aiming for consistent volume and tone. Once you are comfortable, use a metronome clicking quarter notes to gauge your rhythmic accuracy.

Fingerstyle, keep alternating between index (i) and middle (m) fingers. Pick style, observe the downstroke (⊓) and upstroke (V) indications shown.

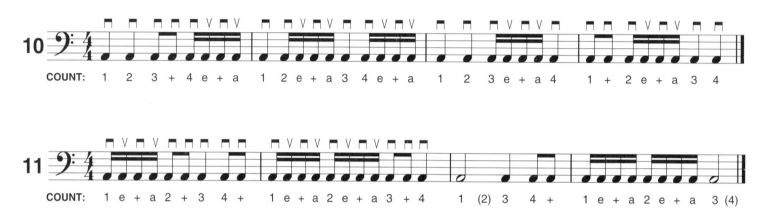

10

COUNT: 1 2 3 + 4 e + a   1 2 e + a 3 4 e + a   1 2 3 e + a 4   1 + 2 e + a 3 4

11

COUNT: 1 e + a 2 + 3 4 +   1 e + a 2 e + a 3 + 4   1 (2) 3 4 +   1 e + a 2 e + a 3 (4)

The quarter note can be broken up many ways using sixteenths. When an eighth and two sixteenths are combined, it is helpful at first to count the silent sixteenth ("ee") during the eighth note.

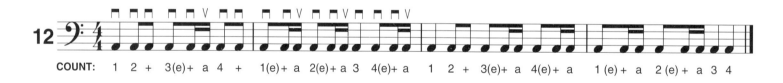

12

COUNT: 1 2 + 3(e)+ a 4 +   1(e)+ a 2(e)+ a 3 4(e)+ a   1 2 + 3(e)+ a 4(e)+ a   1 (e)+ a 2 (e)+ a 3 4

The same is true for two sixteenths and an eighth.

13

COUNT: 1 2 e +(a)3 4   1 e +(a)2 3 e +(a)4   1 + 2 e +(a)3 4 +   1 + 2 e +(a)3 e +(a)4

ONE DROP

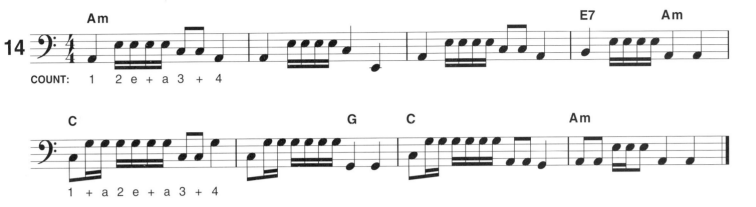

COUNT: 1 2 e + a 3 + 4

1 + a 2 e + a 3 + 4

DADA DADAT

JOG WHEEL

SIXTEENTH RESTS

Sixteenth rests take up the same space as sixteenth notes. They look similar to eighth rests, but they have a double flag (instead of a single) to match the double flag of a sixteenth note.

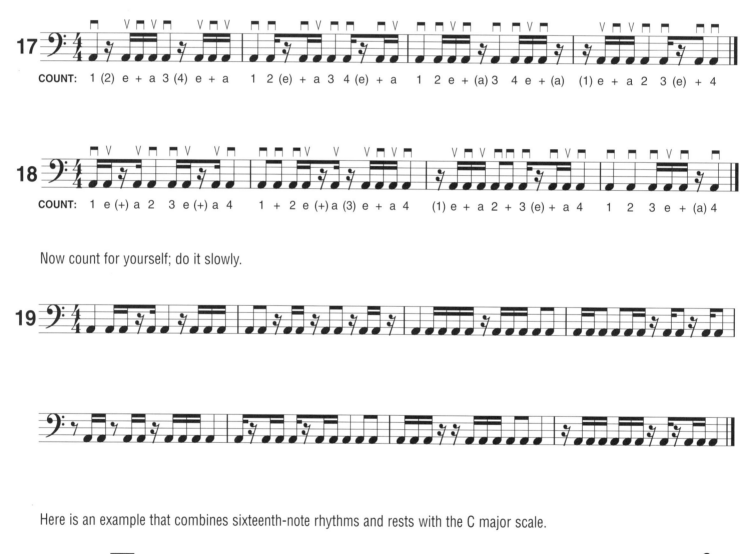

To play sixteenth rests, you'll need to stop the string from vibrating. Use the same technique you used to play staccato: first play a note with either the index (i) or middle (m) finger; then place the alternate finger on the string and stop the vibration. If playing pickstyle, use your left hand to mute the string (observe the picking indications shown).

Now count for yourself; do it slowly.

Here is an example that combines sixteenth-note rhythms and rests with the C major scale.

Notice the sixteenth-note **anticipation** in the last measure; the E is played slightly ahead of the beat.

LAYIN' BACK

Keep track of the missing downbeats; it will help you hit the sixteenth-note offbeats with greater assurance.

NAZZ - T

PLUTONIC

FUNKY SIXTEENTH-NOTE SYNCOPATION

Syncopated sixteenth notes are the essence of funk, Latin, and rock music. Though they are challenging to look at, the rhythms are very familiar to the ear. The key is learning to recognize the sound that matches the picture.

This rhythm uses a **dotted eighth note** and a sixteenth. Remember that a *dot* equals one half of whatever value it is placed after. So a dotted eighth note equals the value of one eighth plus a sixteenth (or three sixteenths).

An easy way to remember this rhythm is to give it a name that sounds like it. Call it "oo-(ka-chu)-bop."

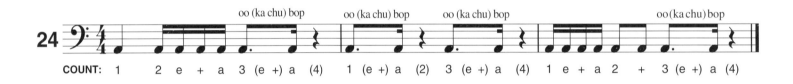

OOKACHU WHA?

A version of "ookachubop" uses a **dotted eighth rest** and a sixteenth note. Say the "ookachu" silently; it will help you play it correctly. This rhythm can be used alone as an upbeat syncopation, or in front of another note as a "pickup" beat.

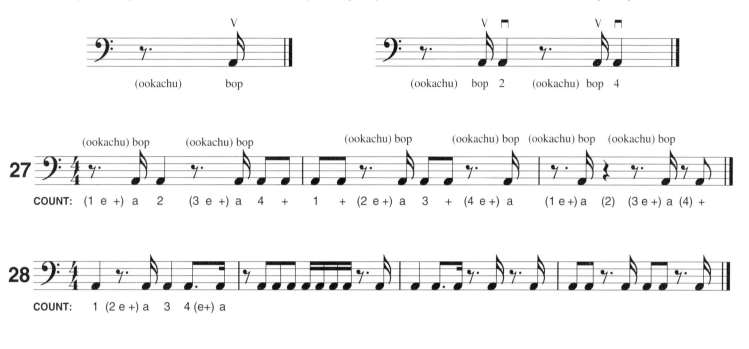

COUNT: (1 e +) a 2 (3 e +) a 4 + 1 + (2 e +) a 3 + (4 e +) a (1 e +) a (2) (3 e +) a (4) +

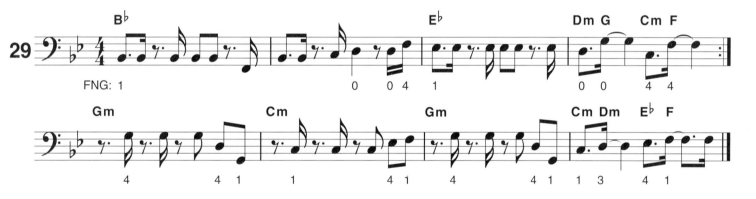

COUNT: 1 (2 e +) a 3 4 (e +) a

GROOVE

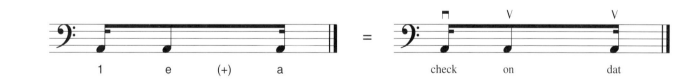

Call this new rhythm "check-on-dat."

COUNT: 1 e (+) a (2) 3 e (+) a 4 + 1 e + a 2 e (+) a 3 + 4 e (+) a 1 + 2 e (+) a 3 e (+) a 4

COUNT: 1 e (+) a 2 (e+) a 3 + 4

COMBO

This next rhythm is similar to "check on dat"; it hits on the "e" and "a" of the beat. Call it "(chk) got - dot"; the (chk) is spoken as a place marker but not played.

(1) e (+) a

(chk) got - dot

MINOR GLITCH

This rhythm hits on the downbeat and the "e." A good name for it is "chick-en."

A variation of "chick-en" uses a rest on the downbeat, making the "chick" silent.

It's interesting to combine the "names" for different rhythms. Creating rhythmic "sentences" like this can help you remember tricky rhythms and play them with assurance. When you first look through this example, see how many rhythm "names" you can identify.

DO IT NOW

When taking the repeat back to measure 1, play the low G with the first finger. Switch back to open when you play the A.

SOUL GROOVE

D - TROIT

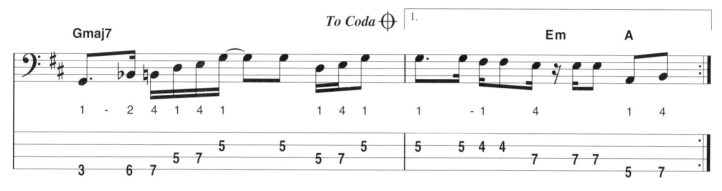

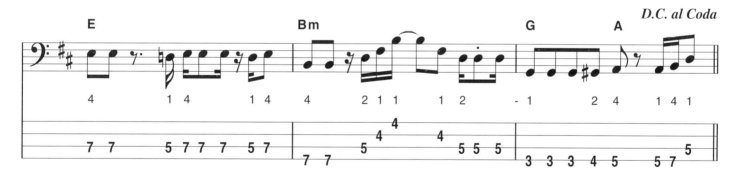

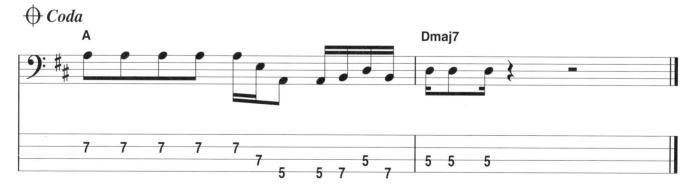

SEVENTH CHORDS

Seventh chords are four-note structures that contain the familiar major and minor triads—root, 3rd, and 5th—plus one more note, the 7th. There are several types of seventh chord; we'll look at the three most common.

MAJOR SEVENTH

The major seventh chord is built 1-3-5-7. The chord symbol is written as "maj7," though some books write it as "M7" or "Δ7". There is a universal fingering for the major seventh chord that allows you to play it in any key.

When you practice these arpeggios, become familiar with the specific note names that "spell" each chord. Try the universal fingering, as well as open fingerings where indicated.

FLOATY

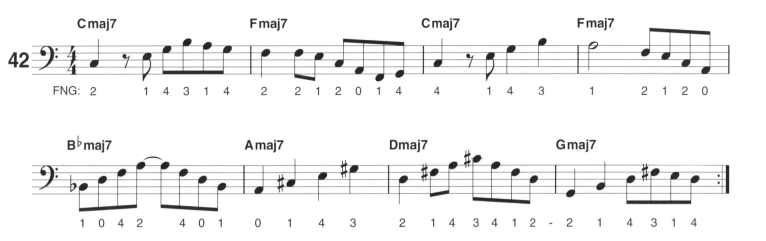

The tablature will help you find the best positions for this example, but experiment with other ways to play it.

VANILLA

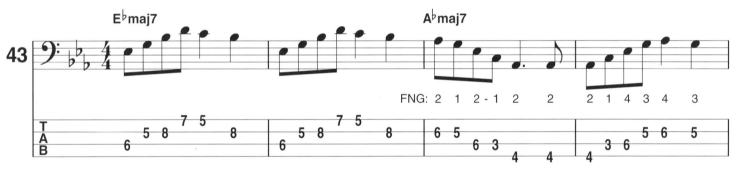

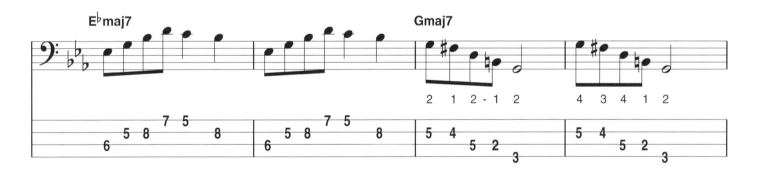

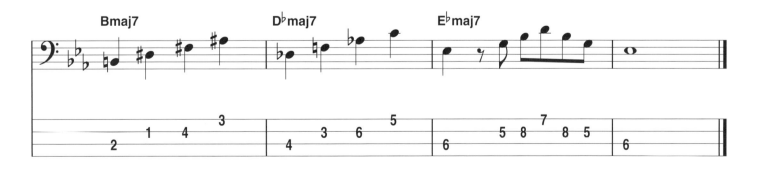

DOMINANT SEVENTH

Dominant seventh chords are also known simply as "7" chords, as in "G7" or "A7."

They are built 1-3-5-♭7, and the universal fingering is 2-1-4-2.

Remember to learn the names of the notes in each chord, and find alternate fingerings. Practice the universal fingering, as well as open fingerings, where indicated.

The blues is always full of dominant seventh chords; here is a classic example of how to use the arpeggio to create a bass line.

LI'L THING

FUNK TIME

MINOR SEVENTH

Minor seventh chords are built 1-♭3-5-♭7. They can be written "m7" as in "Am7" (or "min7" as in "Amin7").

There are two universal fingerings for a minor seventh chord; they are best illustrated with Am7.

Say the note names aloud as you play each arpeggio. Try both universal fingerings, and open fingerings where indicated.

LITTLE M

This piece is played with a shuffle, or swing, feel. Be sure to play the eighth notes "unevenly"—i.e., as if they were the first and third notes of a triplet. The shuffle indication () tells you this.

SHUFFLIN'

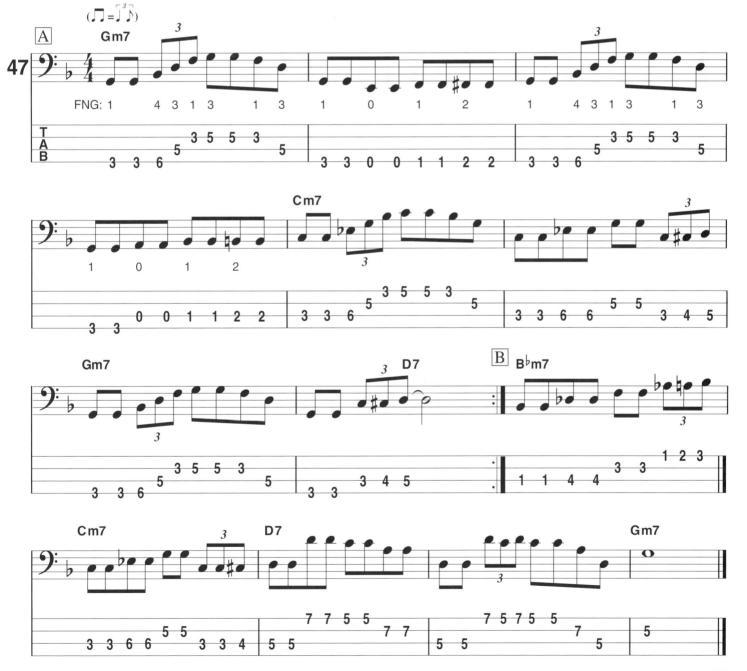

These examples combine the different seventh chords.

MIDDLE MAN

ON THE VERGE

SLIDES

Sliding into a note is a great way to give your bass line personality. It can sound relaxed and loose, or create a dramatic effect. When sliding from one note to another, slightly relax the pressure on the slide finger to avoid making the fret sound too pronounced. Practice sliding with different fingers, at various speeds, and different distances. If a slide has a "slur" marking above it, only the first note is plucked; the second note is simply slid into.

SLIPPIN' & SLIDIN'

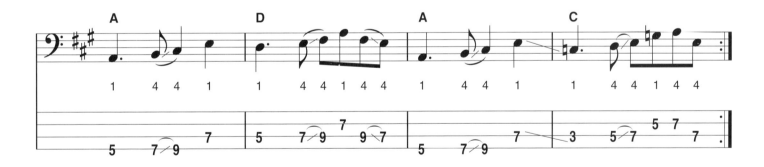

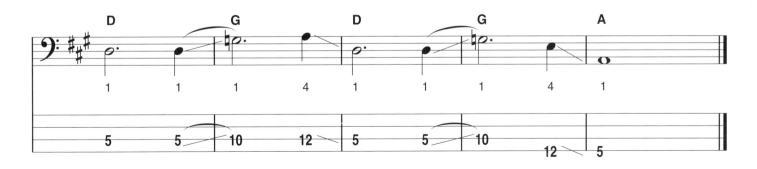

MINOR PENTATONIC

Pentatonic scales are five-note structures that are widely used in all styles of music. The **minor pentatonic** scale is built 1-♭3-4-5-♭7-8 (the octave is not counted as a separate note; hence the name penta-tonic).

There are two universal fingerings. The first is based on the minor scale position and uses one finger per fret; the second uses the 1-2-4 fingering system and starts on the 4th finger, shifting up between scale degrees 4 and 5.

A MINOR PENTATONIC

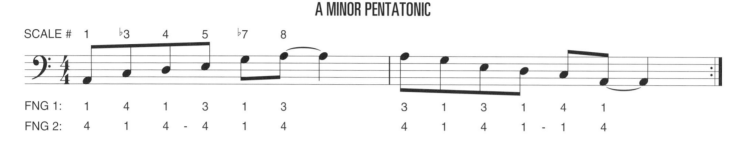

Here are the most common keys for the minor pentatonic scale. E minor pentatonic is in open position and has a unique fingering; the rest use the universal fingerings shown above. Optional open position fingerings are also indicated in some cases.

E MINOR PENT.   B MINOR PENT.

F# MINOR PENT.   C# MINOR PENT.

G# MINOR PENT.   D MINOR PENT.

G MINOR PENT.   C MINOR PENT.

F MINOR PENT.   B♭ MINOR PENT.

The minor pentatonic scale works well when you have to "jam" or improvise on one chord. This example shows you how to play up and down the scale in G and C.

VENTURE FORTH

This example uses a repetitive minor pentatonic idea or "lick" and moves it around to match the chord changes.

DEJA VIEW

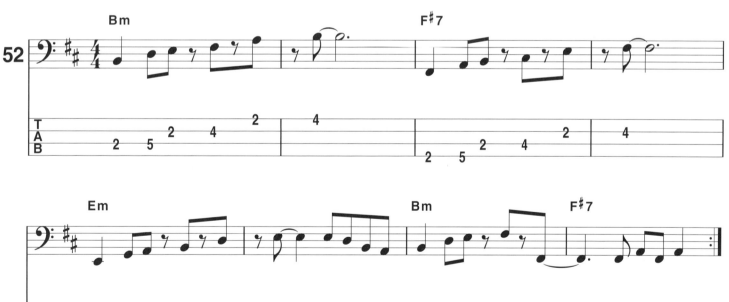

HAMMER-ONS & PULL-OFFS

Two adjacent notes on the same string can be played with one pluck of the finger using a **hammer-on** or a **pull-off**. Play a lower note with the 1st finger, and then "hammer on" to the higher note with the 4th finger. Reverse this action by playing a higher note with the 4th finger, and then "pull off" to the 1st. These articulations are indicated with a slur marking.

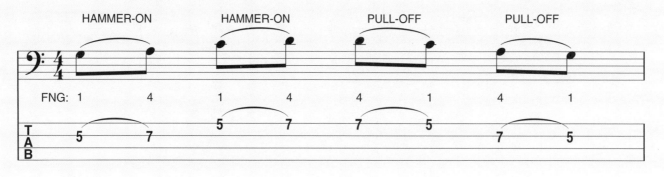

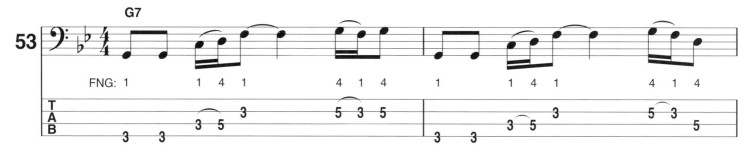

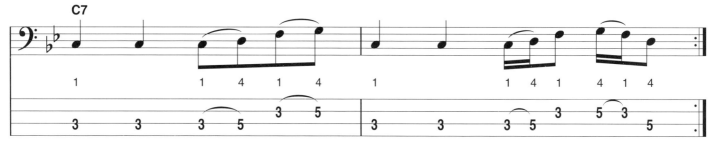

HAMMER HEAD

Here is a two-octave fingering for E minor pentatonic. It uses slides while shifting positions. Notice the slides are in different locations going up and down.

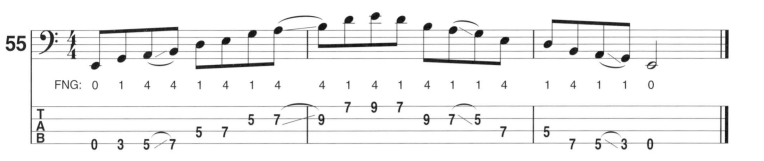

The chord progression of this example follows the notes of the E minor pentatonic scale, a common approach in rock song-writing.

X-TENDER

MAJOR PENTATONIC

The **major pentatonic** scale is also widely used in many styles of music. It is built 1-2-3-5-6-8. There are two universal fingerings. The first follows the major scale position using OFPF; the second uses the 1-2-4 fingering system and starts on the 1st finger, shifting up the string between scale degrees 2 and 3.

C MAJOR PENTATONIC

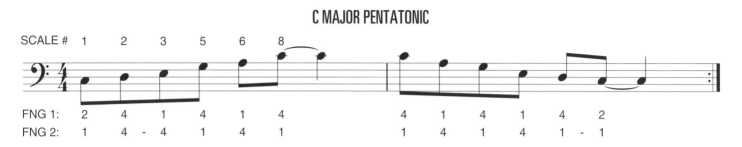

SCALE #	1	2	3	5	6	8		4	1	4	1	4	2
FNG 1:	2	4	1	4	1	4		4	1	4	1	4	2
FNG 2:	1	4	- 4	1	4	1		1	4	1	4	1	- 1

Here are the other common keys for the major pentatonic scale. They can all use the two universal fingerings, except for E and F, which are in open position. G, A, and B♭ are marked with optional open-position fingerings.

G MAJOR PENT.   D MAJOR PENT.

FNG: 2 0 1 0 1 0

A MAJOR PENT.   E MAJOR PENT.

FNG: 0 1 4 1 4 1   0 1 4 1 4 1

B MAJOR PENT.   F MAJOR PENT.

FNG: 1 4 0 4 0 4

B♭ MAJOR PENT.   E♭ MAJOR PENT.

FNG: 1 4 0 4 0 4

A♭ MAJOR PENT.   D♭ MAJOR PENT.

JUST LIKE MY GIRL

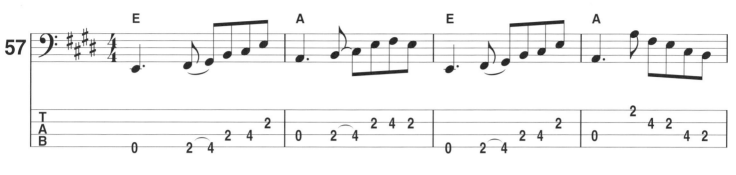

N'AWLINS BEAT

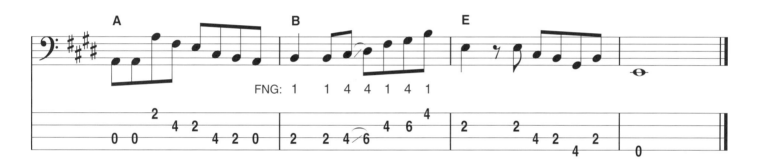

PLAYING OFF CHORD SYMBOLS

While most of what you've learned so far has been written out for you, the bassist is often called upon to create his or her own part or line based on a series of chord symbols. Fortunately, it is fairly simple to create solid, functional bass lines that outline a chord progression using the information you already have at your disposal.

The first priority of a good bass line is to establish the **root motion**—that is, movement from one chord to the next. By using the rhythmic feel of the song and playing the root of each new chord, you can create a perfectly usable bass line that, while not exotic, is often the best thing to play. You'll usually have several possible locations to choose for each root—avoid making jumps bigger than an octave from one root to another.

JUST ROOTS

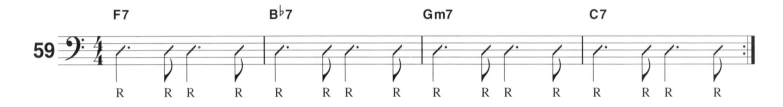

Here is the same chord progression using a steady eighth-note rhythm.

ROOTS & 8THS

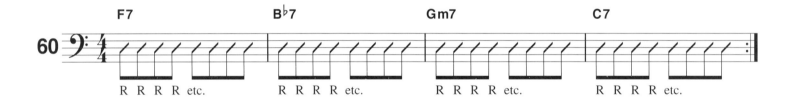

The **octave** is still the root of the chord, but it gives the line a feeling of movement. You can start on the lower root and use the higher octave, or you can reverse this and start on the higher octave and use the low root for movement.

JUMPING OCTAVES

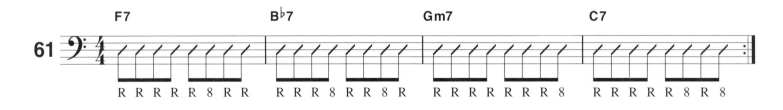

TIP: When playing octaves fingerstyle, it's often easiest to use a "split fingering": middle finger (m) on the higher string and index (i) on the lower. When alternating fingers on a single string with occasional octave jumps, use your middle finger to jump up to the octave, and your index finger to jump down.

Play your own bass line to this chord progression. Using the suggested rhythm, play roots and octaves.

YOUR TURN

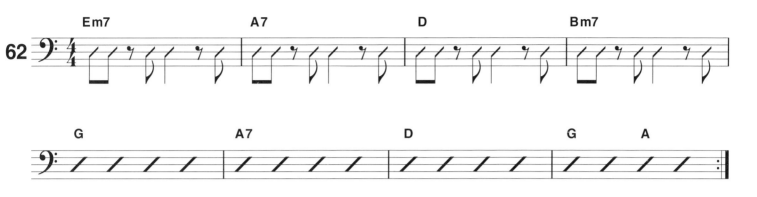

ADDING THE 5TH

The next note to add to a bass line is the **5th** of the chord. An easy way to find the 5th is to go up 2 frets and over one string. But you can also find the 5th *below* the root: it's located at the same fret, one string lower (using the finger roll). For example, C's 5th is G; you can find it above or below the root.

Either high or low 5th will work when creating bass parts; it's up to you to decide which sounds best.

Notice how smooth transitions from one chord to the next can create direction in a line. In this progression, starting on the higher F gives you the option of playing the low 5th, which flows easily into the lower B♭; the high 5th of B♭ moves nicely into the higher G, and so on. It's important to keep this type of close movement in mind when creating your own bass part.

USE THE 5

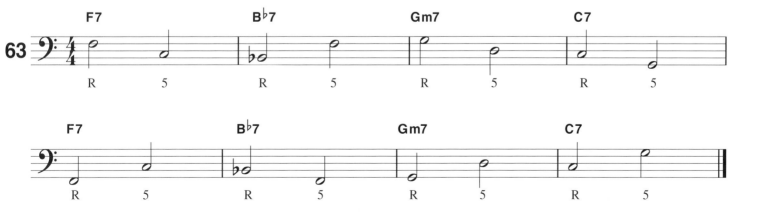

Create your own part using the steady eighth-note rhythm. You can play it through once using the lower root choices, and the next time with the higher ones.

5 BY 8

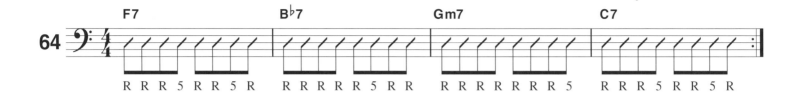

Roots, 5ths, and octaves outline the basic structure of any chord; they are safe choices that work with any chord type. This time, use the root, 5th, and octave together to create a line. Remember that you can start on a low root and move up to the octave, or you can start on a high root and move down to a low octave.

ROOT-5-8

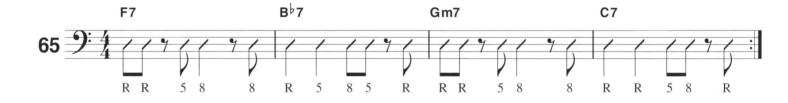

Create your own bass line to this progression using roots, 5ths, and octaves. Use the indicated rhythm, and alternate the line from octave to root on one chord, root to octave on the next. Then see what variations you can find.

YOU GOT IT

CHROMATIC APPROACH

The root, 5th, and octave are **target notes**; you aim for the root on the downbeat of a new chord, while the 5th and octave are two notes that allow for movement during the measure without interfering with the chord type. To create even more movement in the bass line, we add **approach notes**—notes that *lead into* a target note.

Chromatic approach notes lead into the target note by a half step (one fret). They can approach the target from above or below. Notice how this bass line uses a chromatic approach (chr) to lead into the root of each new chord. In measures 3 and 4, a "chr" is also used to lead into the 5th, adding more movement to the line.

When choosing your chromatic approach notes, remember to try them from above *and* below the target note.

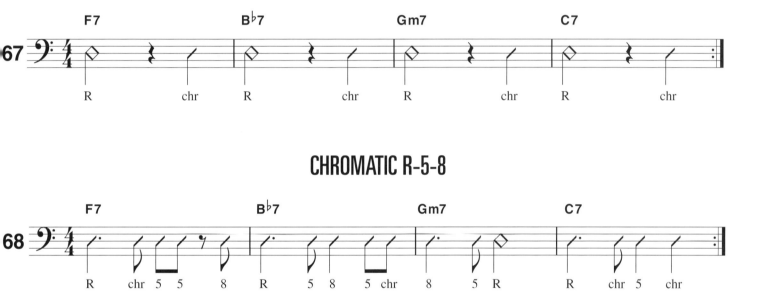

CHROMATIC R-5-8

Now use chromatic approach on your own. Start by simply playing the root and a "chr" to the next chord. When you're comfortable with the progression, add the 5th of each chord. Then use "chr" to lead into those 5ths. Any of the rhythms from previous examples will work; start simply, and then experiment.

IT'S UP TO YOU

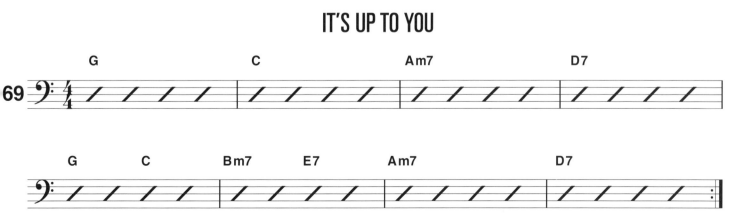

Scale approach uses the adjacent scale tone (from above or below) to approach the target note. Use the scale of the *new* target chord. Most of the time, scale approach is a whole step (2 frets). There are, however, instances where the scale tone may be a half step away from the target—for example, when approaching a major chord from below. It doesn't matter whether you call it scale or chromatic approach; just use it.

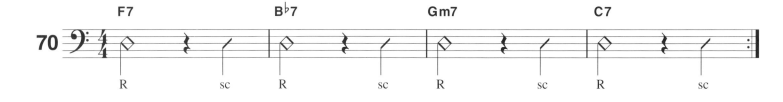

TIP: When approaching a dominant seventh chord (e.g., A7) from below, use a ♭7 scale degree to match the chord.

This uses "sc" to the 5th on the B♭7 and C7. Once you are comfortable with this version, look for other ways to use "sc" with this progression.

SCALE R-5-8

Applying any rhythm previously played, use scale approach to move from one chord to the next. Then try adding the 5th and approaching it when you choose. (Tip: For minor chords, remember to use a ♭6 when approaching the 5th.)

ALL YOURS

DOMINANT APPROACH

Dominant approach uses the 5th of the target note. Many chord progressions are built with dominant root motion, which is when the root motion resolves to a new chord from its 5th. In those cases, using a dominant approach simply outlines the existing root motion. Using "dom" between chords that do *not* have a dominant root motion creates a very strong movement.

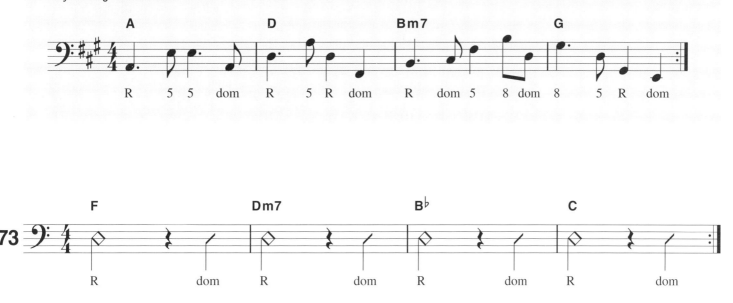

It's tricky at first to grasp using the "dom" of the 5th. This line illustrates the concept effectively. (Hint: It's basically scale degree 2 of the chord.)

DOMINANT TO THE 5TH

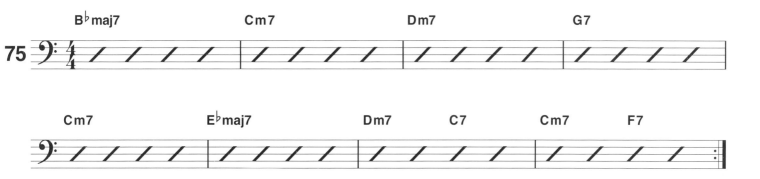

Now use dominant approach on your own. You can add the "dom" that leads into the 5th anytime you want. When the root motion is already dominant, just use the root.

YOU GO, HUGO

USING TRIADS TO CREATE BASS LINES

Triads can be used to build bass lines that clearly state the chord progression. Used in conjunction with the root-5-8 and various approach notes, you have a very complete set of tools to construct an interesting and functional bass part.

The first step is to recognize which *type* of triad the chord symbol indicates. Here are the five basic chord structures you've learned so far. Major and minor triads are easy to grasp; major seventh and dominant seventh chords have major triads as their foundation, while the minor seventh chord contains a minor triad.

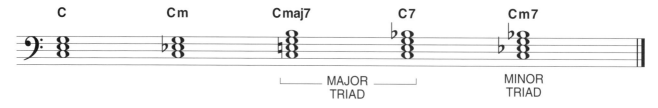

Here is an example of using triads with an approach note to each new chord. Using a quarter-note rhythm, we wind up with a classic walking bass line in a jazz style.

WALKING TRIADS

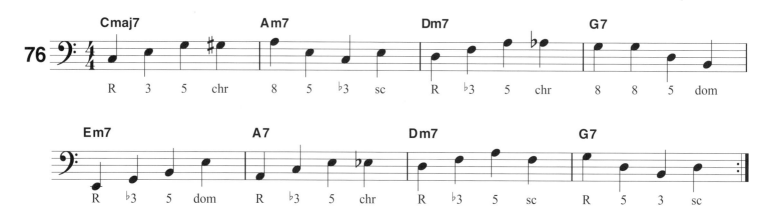

Now it's your turn to walk through the "changes." Stick to triads only at first. You can vary your line by playing the chord tones in a different order and direction.

WALK THIS WAY

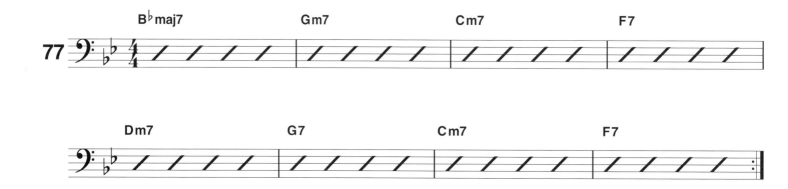

132

It is possible to "bounce around" within the triad—notice that the F triad below changes directions. The second half is open for you to make your own choices; make sure you are familiar with each triad before playing.

SIMPLE TRIADS

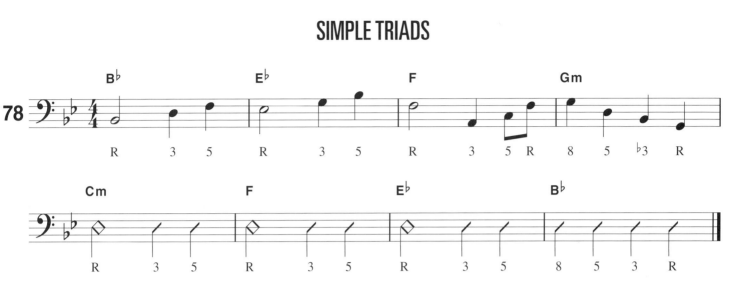

Once you're comfortable with a chord progression, try adding approach notes on beat 4. Remember: you have three ways of approaching a target note: by half step (1 fret), whole step (2 frets), or by 5th. Play the triad for the first three beats of each measure, but focus your attention on the upcoming chord, and play around with different approaches to its root.

ON YOUR OWN

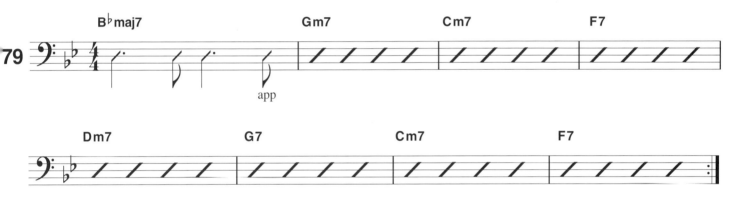

Here's the same chord progression as example 76, played with a dotted quarter/eighth note rhythm. Notice the different ways the triad gets placed in the measure. Also notice the approach notes—nearly all of them are also chord tones! (Can you spot the one that isn't?)

TRIADS & DOTTED QUARTERS

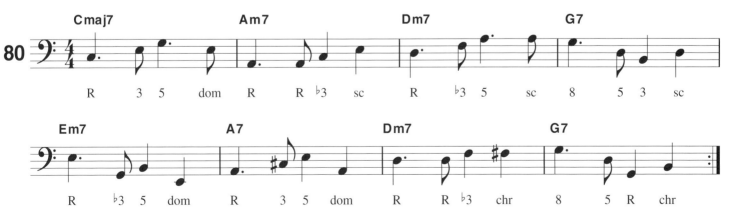

Create your own bass line for this song; use all the methods you've learned so far. Any rhythm will work.

UH HUH

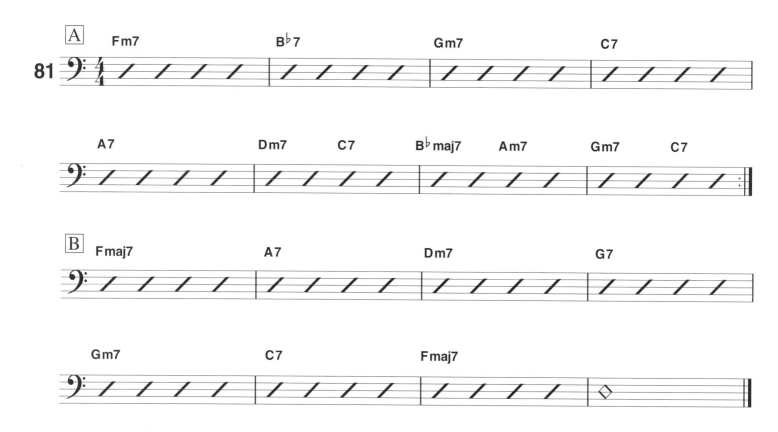

LOCKING IN TO THE GROOVE

A **groove** is any particular rhythmic idea that forms the basis of a song. When bass and drums play together, they need to connect their parts so that it feels like one unified beat. The term "locking in to the groove" is used to describe this phenomenon. To lock in, the bassist and drummer must listen to each other's part and find a shared sense of where the groove is, so they can play together. One way that bassists and drummers connect is by matching the bass line with the kick drum. Examples A and B are two common rhythms you've worked with. Examine the matching drum part, and see how the bass line "hooks up" with the beat.

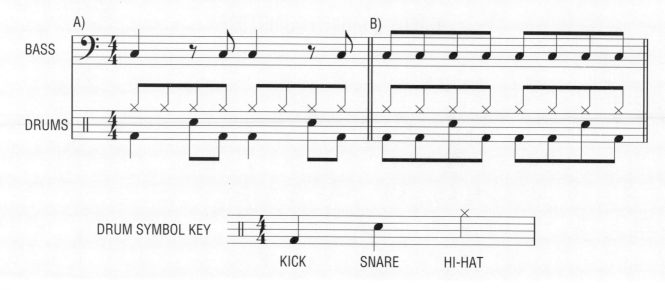

Here are six different rhythms, or grooves. Learn each, then apply it to the chord—in this case, C7. Start by playing only the root; once you've locked in with the groove, see what other notes you can play. Although there are many note choices available, you're not obligated to play them all. However, as a bassist, you are obligated to maintain the groove.

GROOVE JAM

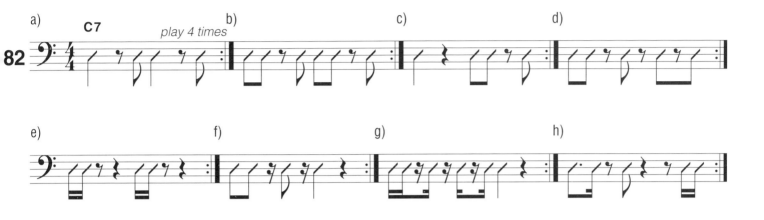

The grooves for the A and B sections are indicated. Use them as the basis for your line. Start with simple ideas that match the rhythm. As you get more comfortable, you'll find it is possible to vary your line within the basic feel and still keep the groove intact. Experiment with different note choices; use root-5-8, chord tones, and different approach notes.

TIME 2 GROOVE

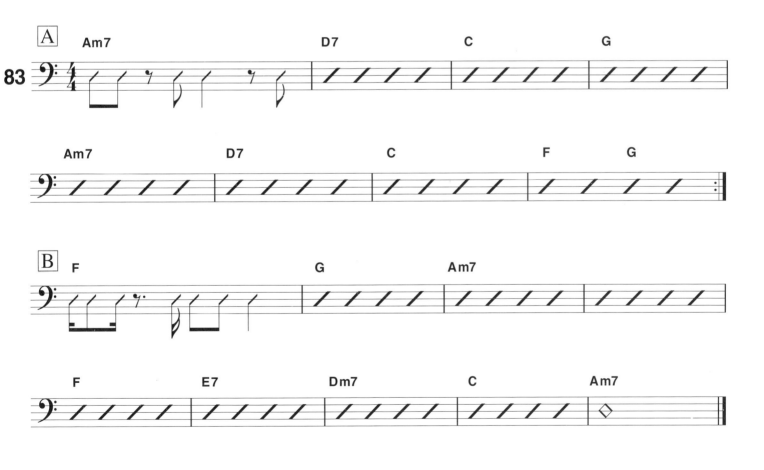

SLAP FUNK

The slap funk style started in the late 1960s and is still one of the most popular techniques that bassists use. The two essential elements of the technique are **slapping** the strings (with the thumb) and **popping** them (with the index and middle fingers).

THE SLAP

Keep the thumb parallel with the string—using the bony knob of your thumb knuckle for the striking surface, hit the string at the end of the fingerboard. Use a twist-like motion in the wrist, and pivot the forearm from the elbow to "whip" the thumb on and off the string. Make sure the thumb "recoils" off the string, allowing it to ring.

TIP: Round wound strings are best for slap funk. Medium to low string height allows the bass to respond to the thumb slap. You don't want to hit the string too hard; it's wasted energy, and it chokes the sound of the note.

Keep the right arm and shoulder loose and relaxed; tension in these areas greatly decreases how funky you can get!

Start by slapping the open strings. Strive for consistent volume and tone for each note, and from string to string. Mute the open strings with the left hand—laying your fingers flat across the strings—in between slaps, but give the note its full value. The slap will be notated using the letter "T" for thumb.

Now practice switching strings; remember to keep the thumb parallel with the string for better accuracy.

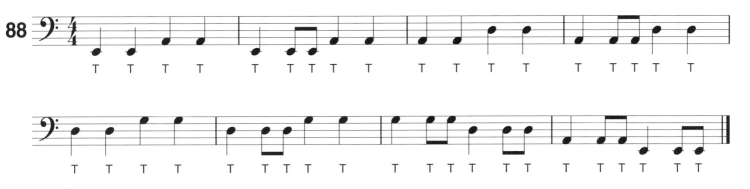

This example requires you to slap up the E and A strings.

SLAP THIS

This example takes you up a two-octave E minor pentatonic scale, a very common structure in slap funk. Strive for consistent volume from string to string.

PENT UP

THE POP

The pop is achieved by pulling the string with the index or middle finger away from the neck, letting it snap back onto the frets. Make a loose fist with your right hand. Let the thumb come to rest against the E string, parallel as if you were going to slap it. Let your index finger naturally fall in between the D and G string, and the middle finger curl under the G. Pull from the side of the finger. Don't get "caught up" in the string; use just enough to pull the string lightly. Too much pull makes the pop louder than needed, and can cause broken strings.

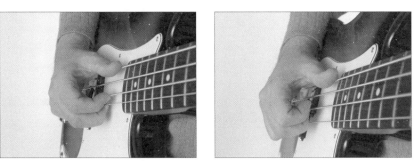

Although it is possible to slap or pop any string, for the most part, you will be slapping the E and A strings and popping the D and G. It works best to dedicate the index (1st) finger to popping the D string and the middle (2nd) finger to the G.

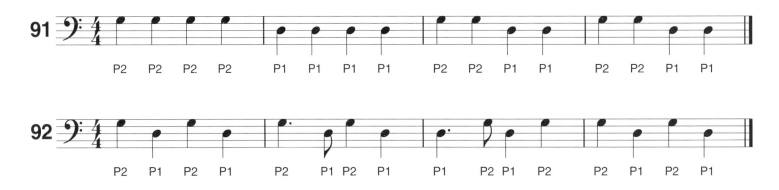

COMBINING SLAP AND POP

Slap the string, prepare to pop

Combining slap and pop into a smooth, two-piece movement is the next step. When you slap the string, move your finger into position for the pop. Let the thumb recoil from the slap without moving your hand away from the string, then slip the pop finger under the string and pull/release.

After slap, pop the string

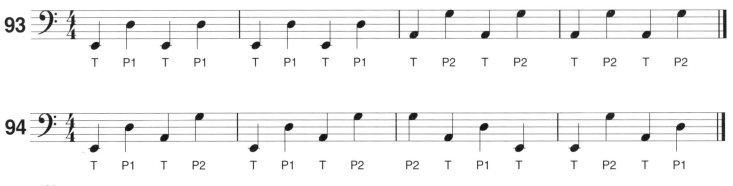

The octave is a very common part of slap funk. Practice playing these octaves with alternating slap and pop.

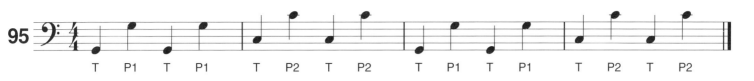

When play the octave C's, try letting the tip of your index finger mute the low E string.

OCTAVE SLAP

This exercise moves the slap/pop octave around the fingerboard. As usual, play the octave with the 1st and 4th fingers (left hand), but when you play the open E and A strings, use the 2nd finger for their octaves.

CHROMATIC OCTAVES

This rhythmic variation helps develop thumb control.

GRITTY

THE PRESSURE ROLL

The hammer-on is a technique you already know that's used often in slap funk. Sometimes, it's necessary to set up a hammer-on with the use of a **pressure roll** across the strings. Play a low G with the tip of the 1st finger as usual. Now *roll* the pressure used to push the string down, across to the D string, without dropping the tip of the fin-

Playing with tip

Pressure roll

ger; you'll play the F on the 3rd fret, D string with the bottom part of the 1st finger. This pressure roll allows you to smoothly jump across the strings between slap and pop.

Now use the pressure roll to set up the hammer-ons (indicated with a slur) from the 1st finger to the 4th.

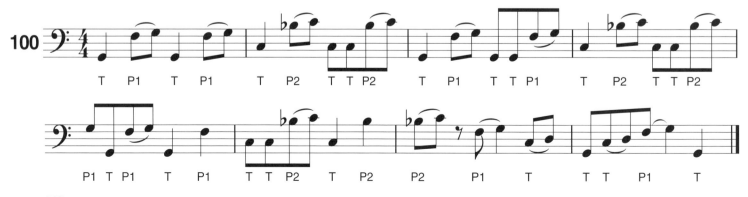

This example uses a pull-off as well as the hammer-on.

DEAD NOTES

Dead notes are an important part of the slap funk style. By not pushing the string all the way down to the fretboard (in the left hand), you produce a note that is not a true pitch. Slapping or popping these notes creates a unique percussive effect that blends in well.

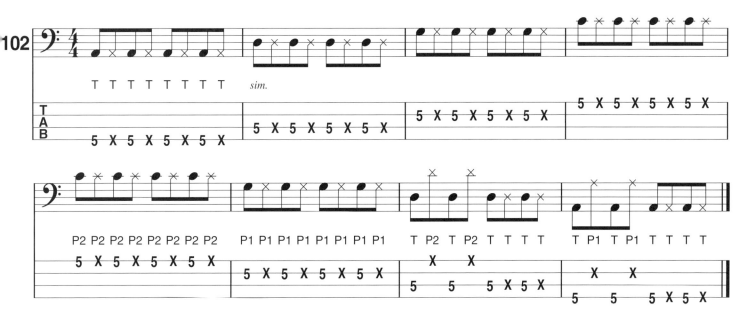

DEAD END

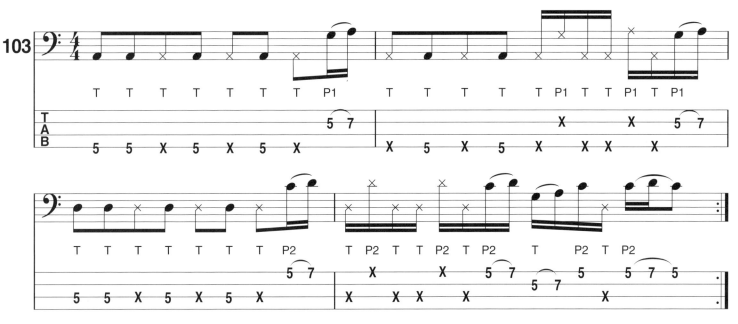

The A section requires you to create your own bass line from the chord symbols and rhythm, while the B section has a specific slap funk line to play. It may take some practice to get comfortable switching from fingerstyle to slap; make sure you stay aware of the switch-over point in the song. The last two measures of the coda are played fingerstyle.

KEEP IT TOGETHER

This one is a busy sixteenth-note tune with some technical challenges. Be sure to keep your tempo consistent.

IT'S AN EYEFUL!

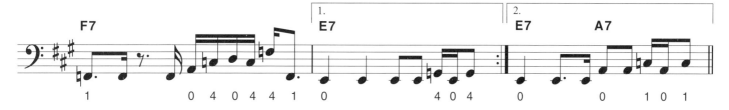

HAL LEONARD
BASS METHOD

METHOD BOOKS

by Ed Friedland

BOOK 1 - 2ND EDITION
Book 1 teaches: tuning; playing position; musical symbols; notes within the first five frets; common bass lines, patterns and rhythms; rhythms through eighth notes; playing tips and techniques; more than 100 great songs, riffs and examples; and more! The audio includes 44 full-band tracks for demonstration or play-along.
00695067 Book Only.................................. $9.99
00695068 Book/Online Audio.............................. $14.99
01100122 Deluxe - Book/Online Audio/Video $19.99

BOOK 2 - 2ND EDITION
Book 2 continues where Book 1 left off and teaches: the box shape; moveable boxes; notes in fifth position; major and minor scales; the classic blues line; the shuffle rhythm; tablature; and more!
00695069 Book Only.................................. $9.99
00695070 Book/Online Audio.............................. $14.99

BOOK 3 - 2ND EDITION
With the third book, progressing students will learn more great songs, riffs and examples; sixteenth notes; playing off chord symbols; slap and pop techniques; hammer-ons and pull-offs; playing different styles and grooves; and more.
00695071 Book Only.............................. $9.99
00695072 Book/Online Audio.............................. $14.99

COMPOSITE - 2ND EDITION
This money-saving edition contains Books 1, 2 and 3.
00695073 Book Only........................... $19.99
00695074 Book/Online Audio.............................. $27.99

DVD
Play your favorite songs in no time with this DVD! Covers: tuning, notes in first through third position, rhythms through eighth notes, fingerstyle and pick playing, 4/4 and 3/4 time, and more! Includes 6 full songs and on-screen music notation. 68 minutes.
00695849 DVD.................................... $19.95

BASS FOR KIDS
by Chad Johnson
Bass for Kids is a fun, easy course that teaches children to play bass guitar faster than ever before. Popular songs such as "Crazy Train," "Every Breath You Take," "A Hard Day's Night" and "Wild Thing" keep kids motivated, and the clean, simple page layouts ensure their attention remains focused on one concept at a time.
00696449 Book/Online Audio $14.99

REFERENCE BOOKS

BASS SCALE FINDER
by Chad Johnson
Learn to use the entire fretboard with the *Bass Scale Finder*. This book contains over 1,300 scale diagrams for the most important 17 scale types.
00695781 6" x 9" Edition.......................................$9.99
00695778 9" x 12" Edition..................................$10.99

BASS ARPEGGIO FINDER
by Chad Johnson
This extensive reference guide lays out over 1,300 arpeggio shapes. 28 different qualities are covered for each key, and each quality is presented in four different shapes.
00695817 6" x 9" Edition.......................................$9.99
00695816 9" x 12" Edition.....................................$9.99

MUSIC THEORY FOR BASSISTS
by Sean Malone
Acclaimed bassist and composer Sean Malone will explain the written language of music, using easy-to-understand terms and concepts, diagrams, and much more. The audio provides 96 tracks of examples, demonstrations, and play-alongs.
00695756 Book/Online Audio $19.99

STYLE BOOKS

BASS LICKS
by Ed Friedland
This comprehensive supplement to any bass method will help students learn over 200 great bass licks, lines and grooves in many rhythmic styles. *Bass Licks* illustrates how simple melodic patterns can become the springboard for group improvisation or the foundation of a song.
00696035 Book/Online Audio $15.99

BASS LINES
by Matt Scharfglass
500 expertly written bass lines, riffs and fills in a wide variety of musical genres are included in this comprehensive collection to help players expand their bass vocabulary. The examples cover many tempos, keys and feels, and include easy bass lines for beginners on up to advanced riffs for more experienced bassists.
00148194 Book/Online Audio $22.99

BLUES BASS
by Ed Friedland
Learn to play studying the songs of B.B. King, Stevie Ray Vaughan, Muddy Waters, Albert King, the Allman Brothers, T-Bone Walker, and many more. Learn riffs from blues classics including: Born Under a Bad Sign • Hideaway • Hoochie Coochie Man • Killing Floor • Pride and Joy • Sweet Home Chicago • The Thrill Is Gone • and more.
00695870 Book/Online Audio $17.99

COUNTRY BASS
by Glenn Letsch
21 songs, including: Act Naturally • Boot Scootin' Boogie • Crazy • Honky Tonk Man • Love You Out Loud • Luckenbach, Texas (Back to the Basics of Love) • No One Else on Earth • Ring of Fire • Southern Nights • Streets of Bakersfield • Whose Bed Have Your Boots Been Under? • and more.
00695928 Book/Online Audio $22.99

FRETLESS BASS
by Chris Kringel
18 songs, including: Bad Love • Continuum • Even Flow • Everytime You Go Away • Hocus Pocus • I Could Die for You • Jelly Roll • King of Pain • Kiss of Life • Lady in Red • Tears in Heaven • Very Early • What I Am • White Room • more.
00695850..$22.99

FUNK BASS
by Chris Kringel
This is your complete guide to learning the basics of grooving and soloing funk bass. Songs include: Can't Stop • I'll Take You There • Let's Groove • Stay • What Is Hip • and more.
00695792 Book/Online Audio.............................. $22.99

R&B BASS
by Glenn Letsch
This book/audio pack uses actual classic R&B, Motown, soul and funk songs to teach you how to groove in the style of James Jamerson, Bootsy Collins, Bob Babbitt, and many others. The 19 songs include: For Once in My Life • Knock on Wood • Mustang Sally • Respect • Soul Man • Stand by Me • and more.
00695823 Book/Online Audio $19.99

ROCK BASS
by Sean Malone
This book/audio pack uses songs from a myriad of rock genres to teach the key elements of rock bass. Includes: Another One Bites the Dust • Beast of Burden • Money • Roxanne • Smells like Teen Spirit • and more.
00695801 Book/Online Audio..............................$22.99

SUPPLEMENTARY SONGBOOKS

These great songbooks correlate with Books 1-3 of the *Hal Leonard Bass Method*, giving students great songs to play while they're still learning! The audio tracks include great accompaniment and demo tracks.

EASY POP BASS LINES
20 great songs that students in Book 1 can master. Includes: Come as You Are • Crossfire • Great Balls of Fire • Imagine • Surfin' U.S.A. • Takin' Care of Business • Wild Thing • and more.
00695809 Book/Online Audio..............................$16.99

MORE EASY POP BASS LINES
20 great songs for Level 2 students. Includes: Bad, Bad Leroy Brown • Crazy Train • I Heard It Through the Grapevine • My Generation • Pride and Joy • Ramblin' Man • Summer of '69 • and more.
00695819 Book Only...$14.99
00695818 Book/Online Audio..............................$16.99

EVEN MORE EASY POP BASS LINES
20 great songs for Level 3 students, including: ABC • Another One Bites the Dust • Brick House • Come Together • Higher Ground • Iron Man • The Joker • Sweet Emotion • Under Pressure • more.
00695821 Book...$14.99
00695820 Book/Online Audio..............................$16.99

Visit Hal Leonard online at
www.halleonard.com